LOVE LETTERS TO MISCARRIAGE MOMS

You Are Not Alone

You Are Not Alone: Grieve with Hope Series

Lee Ann~
What a beautiful
soul, you are.
And what an
amazing story.
All the blessings,
Sam Evans

Samantha Evans

Blackside Publishing
Colorado Springs, CO

Connect with Samantha (Sam) Evans

Email and Newsletter Sign-up:
Sam@LoveSamEvans.com

Amazon Author Central:
www.amazon.com/author/LoveSamEvans

Facebook: Love Sam Evans:
www.facebook.com/groups/LoveSamEvans

Facebook: Miscarriage Support: www.facebook.com/LoveLetterstoMiscarriage-MomsSupportGroup

Instagram: www.instagram.com/LoveSamEvans/
LinkedIn: www.linkedin.com/LoveSamEvans
Twitter: www.twitter.com/LoveSamEvans
Website/Blog: www.LovesSamEvans.com

Publisher's Note: The memoir reflections in this book are the author's present recollections of experiences over time. Some names and characteristics were changed to protect those who asked to remain anonymous, some events were compressed, and some dialogue was recreated.

Scripture quotations marked (AMP) are taken from the (NASB®) New American Standard Bible®, Copyright © 1960, 1971, 1977, 1995, 2020 by The Lockman Foundation. Used by permission. All rights reserved. www.lockman.org
Scripture marked (ERV) are taken from the Holy Bible: Easy-to-Read Version (ERV), International Edition © 2013, 2016 by Bible League International and used by permission.
Scripture marked (ESV) are taken from The Holy Bible, English Standard Version® (ESV®) Copyright © 2001 by Crossway, a publishing ministry of Good News Publishers. All rights reserved. ESV Text Edition: 2016
Scripture marked (ICB) are taken from the International Children's Bible®. Copyright © 1986, 1988, 1999 by Thomas Nelson. Used by permission. All rights reserved.
Scripture quotations marked MSG are taken from THE MESSAGE, copyright © 1993, 2002, 2018 by Eugene H. Peterson. Used by permission of NavPress, represented by Tyndale House Publishers. All rights reserved.
Scripture quotations marked NASB are taken from the (NASB®) New American Standard Bible®, Copyright © 1960, 1971, 1977, 1995, 2020 by The Lockman Foundation. Used by permission. All rights reserved. www.lockman.org
Scripture quotations marked (NIV) are taken from the Holy Bible, New International Version®, NIV®. Copyright © 1973, 1978, 1984, 2011 by Biblica, Inc.™ Used by permission of Zondervan. All rights reserved worldwide. www.zondervan.comThe "NIV" and "New International Version" are trademarks registered in the United States Patent and Trademark Office by Biblica, Inc.™
Scripture marked (NKJV) are taken from the New King James Version®. Copyright © 1982 by Thomas Nelson. Used by permission. All rights reserved.
Scripture quotations marked (TLB) are taken from The Living Bible copyright © 1971. Used by permission of Tyndale House Publishers, Carol Stream, Illinois 60188. All rights reserved.

Developmental Editor, Researcher, and Writer: Scoti Domeij
Book Design: Scoti Domeij
Cover Photo Credits: tamara-bellis-ZQMTPyuOePw-unsplash; linnea-herner-myl1_IAFeT4-unsplash; hipster-mum-102826-unsplash; szabo-viktor-28ZbKOWiZfs-unsplash; abigail-keenan-99C5lrAyxpQ-unsplash

Blackside Publishing: www.blacksidepublishing.com
Ordering Information: Ingram and Online E-tailers.
Quantity Sales. Special discounts are available on quantity purchases by corporations, associations, and others. For details, email the "Special Sales Department" at BlacksidePublishing@gmail.com.

You Are Not Alone: Love Letters to Miscarriage Moms / Samantha Evans -- 2nd ed.
ISBN 978-1-68355-022-8; ISBN 1-68355-022-6
Printed in the United States.

The Chapter Line Up

What Others Are Saying

Sam scoops up grieving mothers in her arms with her words of encouragement and validation. This author meets readers right where they are in their grief, allowing them to be angry or devastated or hopeful. Grieving readers will hear Sam's own experience, written skillfully and tenderly straight from her heart, plus many other parents' letters of their losses.—Jill Coates

Love Letters to Miscarriage Moms beautifully speaks with a raw authenticity to the full emotional spectrum experienced in grief. The way Sam (and the other contributors) articulate the joys, sorrows, anger, frustration, numbness, and humor of their experiences provide space for readers to reflect on their own stories. The Appendix: Helpful Tips on How Support Someone Who Experienced a Miscarriage, is a practical resource for those who want to care deeply but aren't quite sure how when no words could ever suffice. It is a worthwhile read for any miscarried mom, dad, or anyone who loves someone who has known that pain.—Jeramy Girard, Chaplin

Been there. If you have recently experienced a miscarriage, you'll find someone who shares your pain and provides hope-filled and practical ways to move forward. If you haven't been there, you'll discover helpful things to say and hurtful words to avoid when someone you know has experienced a miscarriage. Thank you, Sam, for sharing your heart and journey.—Lori Wildenberg, author of Messy Hope: Help Your Child Overcome Anxiety, Depression, or Suicidal Ideation.

I loved the way the author's personality, humanism, and dedication to helping others comes through so strongly. She's managed to provide a power of empathy, understanding, and empowerment that is rare in the books of today's libraries.

Mothers who've suffered a miscarriage will gain hope after reading the author's book. To my knowledge, there is no other resource that is written in such an enjoyable, anecdotal fashion. This book will serve as an emotional, spiritual, and literal lifeline for mothers past, present, and future.

Mothers and fathers who've suffered a miscarriage in their pursuit to become parents should read this book because it offers relief associated from the pains of miscarriage. A close friend who wishes to better understand the pains of this experience would also have their life richly blessed by reading this book.

Sam, I am so thrilled for your inspired and divine work on lifting up those who ever have or ever will endure the trial of miscarriage. Please continue to write and live out your God-given mission to be a source of light and Christlike support to all who associate with you.—Michael, M.D., Mayo Health Systems

Reading this book has helped me tremendously to understand and have more informed empathy for women who've gone through this traumatic experience. I highly recommend this book to everyone, even for those who, like myself, haven't personally had to go through miscarriage. We all have people in our sphere who've lost a little one and need our compassion and love to help them navigate all the emotions. This honest, and practical book sheds a great deal of light into the ways someone can help, as well as the ways and words one ought NOT to do or say!—*Carol Edwards, a grandmom*

Going through the loss of a baby to miscarriage can make one feel alone and that no one can understand what they're going through. You seek out someone or something that can help you feel connected. In Love Letters to Miscarried Moms, Sam shares her loss, so you are not alone in yours. She writes and grants you permission to feel and experience and permission to survive and love.

This book is not only a way to gain insight and understanding into uncovering your pain, but also serves as a tool to help you feel through your feelings with tools like "love reflections," which helps prompt feelings with words from others. The scripture woven throughout the book and Samantha's approachable, authentic conversational tone makes this book like none other I've ever read. What a blessing this book is to all that need it.—*Keri Neal Storm*

You do not have to have suffered the grief of miscarriage to engage with this book in an important way. I recommend this book to anyone who wants to be a more empathetic mother, sister, and friend to those who've dealt with miscarriage. The author has a unique way of helping the reader understand the loss and grief, as well as the hope surrounding these experiences. Her touching storytelling brings to life what so many women deal with. Though I haven't suffered this kind of loss, I feel better equipped to care for those who have.—*Emily Latimer*

Sam Evans writes truth in all its raw and beautiful glory. She digs beneath the surface to reveal what lies hidden and brings emotion into the light where community lives, inviting discourse and compassion—and even laughter. Her words have changed me for the better. Don't miss a word from this transparent, up-and-coming author!—*Debbie Allen, Writer & Freelance Editor*

Hi, I wanted to write to say thank you. I received your book from my dear friend's mom shortly after I miscarried, and as I read your words, it's like I'm reading my own. For some reason, while I was going through the worst few days of it, I would tell people that it's so weird, but I know why I'm going through this. This is the worst pain a woman can go through, and the only people who can comfort me are the ones who say, "I know how you're feeling!" I know I will have to help someone through it someday, too. As sucky as it is that it's so common, it would be worse to go through it with nobody understanding. Your book is such a blessing and helped me understand my feelings. I'm very thankful. I hope you are doing well in the days since. You are an amazing writer, and someone who feels like a friend now.—*Nina Jones*

A woman from my work miscarried and slipped into serious depression. It was really sad. I didn't know how else to help her, so I gave her your book. She said your book was the only thing that helped her. Not only did it pull her out of her depression, she said it also reignited her relationship with God, which had been dormant for some time.—*Anonymous*

Not a fun subject but it is a wonderful book. She walks through her experience and others. It is like having a friend there with you in the pain. I had a hard time opening the book. If you are hurting from the loss of a child, please read this, and let someone be there with you. My husband went out to sea a week after we lost our baby. I was left feeling alone, depressed, and trying to heal and take care of three kids. This book was there letting me know I'm not alone grieving.—Amazon Review, June 2018

It has helped me greatly cope with my miscarriage and also brought me closer to God! Thank you so much for your beautiful healing words.—Amazon Review June 2017

This book has helped me through my two (back-to-back) miscarriages by putting things into perspective. It made me laugh and made me cry and helped me understand. I'd recommend for anyone who is having a difficult time through their own miscarriage/s or to anyone who needs some understanding of what their friend or spouse has or is going through!—Amazon Review, April 2017

I found and ordered this book the day after I lost our first child. My tears fell on the pages of this book, and yet I was able to smile in some of it as Sam is a perfect writer. I was deeply encouraged by her faith, and this book helped me stay grounded in my faith in the midst of my pain.—Amazon Review, October 2014

Excellent. Thank you for your honest, frank description of the horror of miscarriage. And for giving me permission to grieve indefinitely. Losing baby was second worst day of my life, second only to losing my mom. You are an angel, Sam, thank you, thank you, thank you.—Amazon Review, March 2014

What an amazing, loving perspective on the journey of miscarriage. I believe this book can help heal the hearts of those who have gone through this and help them know they are not alone.—Amazon Review, March 2011

I carry your heart with me

(I carry it in my heart)

I am never without it.

–e e cummings

To Kaylynn, Kelly and Trinity, your father's benediction every Sunday.

May the road rise up to meet you.

May the wind be always at your back.

May the sun shine warm upon your face;

the rains fall soft upon your fields and until we meet again,

may God hold you in the palm of His hand.

–A Celtic Blessing

1 *Dear Friend*

I'm sorry, friend. I truly am. No words can describe your unfathomable pain. And yet, for your sake, and for mine, I have to try.

Just like you, I am a miscarriage mother. The child was my first. I possess no birth certificate, no war stories of labor, and nothing to show of my pregnancy. However, this aching loss indicates—I'm a mother.

I remember . . . the first time I felt light-headed . . . the first time I noticed soreness under my ribs from my body rearranging itself. I remember the funniest birth announcement responses, the first person who prayed for my baby, and printing the "congratulations" I received on Facebook. I remember the photos I snapped of my pregnancy test and progress pictures revealing what no one could see—my baby transforming the shape of my body. I even wrote to my unborn child in a journal.

Surreal.

Devastating.

How can I describe this pain shredding my heart? No language contains enough expletives. I'm left with nothing more to say to you than, "I'm sorry. So, so sorry."

Losing my baby played through my memory like a nightmare stuck on a repeating track. I needed to know I wasn't alone. For two days I

The Lord is close to those who have suffered disappointment. He saves those who are discouraged.

Psalm 34:18.

ERV

only spoke to women who endured a miscarriage. I was furious at unfit mothers whose carelessness resulted in pregnancy . . . who later treated their children like inconveniences. I could hardly speak to women who did not share this tragedy. Their good fortune triggered a torrent of tears—as if my loss required any prompting.

Like shards of a stained-glass window on the cast iron tub beneath my feet, dreams I constructed around my child shattered.

Yet, through the broken fragments, God's character reflected up at me. He could use my loss to help others. I balked at the thought.

"No!" That word melted into pitiful sobs. "Please, no. I don't want to help other people who've gone through this! I don't want compassion for miscarriage moms! I don't want this!" I yelled as blood swirled down the shower drain. May tears mingled with the water streaming down my face.

I hope you understand my outburst. Your loss deserves selfless empathy and an agape depth of unconditional compassion. I didn't want to provide support, because the prerequisite for a merited compassion was the death of my child.

The God of compassion, however, rearranges the pieces of our brokenness into masterfully designed mosaics. The day after I miscarried, God laid this phrase, a title, *Love Letters to Miscarriage Moms* on my heart.

One sobering thought breached my grief: Do grieving mothers know God loves them? *God can use my loss.* As a result, I undertook the task to write this book, and to interview other women who experienced the emotional and physical trauma of miscarriage.

I credit much of my survival to friend-heroes and fellow miscarriage moms. Maybe you'll find a story similar to yours among the women who upheld me throughout my process of mourning. After you record your thoughts in *Reflection: What's on my Heart?*, perhaps you'll receive comfort from *In the Words of Others*, love letters written by men and women who mourned losses like yours. The mini-biographies of women I interviewed appear in *Acknowledgments: Meet the Cast*.

This 10-year anniversary edition also includes an appendix, *Helpful Tips on How to Support Someone Who Experienced a Miscarriage*.

Your story is unique. Your experience was horrific. You're not alone. Grieve with us. Cry with us. Throw tantrums with us. If you choose to throw things with us, we prefer your projectiles aren't aimed at people.

This difficult journey toward healing involves bravery. Only members of our tribe comprehend our unwanted losses and our raw and gruesome ordeal.

My cast of miscarriage moms and I don't require words or descriptions. While the details and circumstances of our stories differ, our losses feel the same.

Each miscarriage mom reiterated a charge to me, that I repeat to you: "Allow yourself to grieve the loss."

After walking alongside our stories, I hope and pray you'll gain inner strength to navigate out of the dark, lonely forest of your grief and move toward the warm light of hope—and maybe even

gain a literary friend along the way. We'll survive this together.

For readers who haven't experienced miscarriage and desire insight into your friend's pain, thank you. You're a rock star. I wrote the *Appendix: Helpful Tips on How to Support Someone Who Experienced a Miscarriage* especially for you.

Reflection: What's On My Heart?

Writing *Love Letters to Miscarriage Moms* helped me cope with my loss and I hope our stories help you to cope with your grief. Let's find our way out of this darkness together.

You are one out of four pregnancies.

You are not alone.

You are loved.

This book is a love letter from my heart to yours.

How you choose to use this space is up to you. Some mourners prefer to process their thoughts and feelings through expressive journaling. Others pause and find solace through art, pens, and colors.

Some prefer to leave a bread trail of clues in the margins of the pages as they wander and stumble through the mourning maze. Science has found that expressing and confessing your thoughts and feelings decreases stress, heals emotional wounds, improves relationships and overall well-being. The outpouring even boosts your immune system.

May God bless you and keep you and meet you within these pages as you navigate your loss your way.

2 Sam I Am

$\mathcal{B}$*efore we talk about* one of the worst days of your life, may I introduce myself to you? I'm Sam. Just Sam.

I was born and raised in Chicagoland.

Pause.

I'm compelled to clear up a few misunderstandings. Chicagoland is not an actual city, only the colloquial term for all suburbs surrounding Chicago. Its nickname, the "Windy City," derives from a long-winded politician, not actual wind.

No suburbs lie east of Chicago—just a lake. A big lake. All stereotypes about traffic are true. Also, the answer to the question, "Sox or Cubs?" stirs more fervor than a presidential debate.

Unpause.

So, Chicagoland. I grew up in Berwyn and remember watching the '85 Bears with my dad—the year running back Walter Payton, quarterback Jim McMahon, and Coach Mike Ditka won the super bowl. I watched Michael Jordan play basketball and stood amidst the chaos of Chicagoland six times when the Chicago Bulls won the World Championship in the 90's.

During my sophomore year at Naperville Central High School, I felt called to ministry. After graduation, I attended University of Northwestern University—St. Paul in Minnesota

"Before I made you in your mother's womb. I knew you.

Before you were born.

I chose you for a special work."

Jeremiah 1:5.
ERV

and majored in Youth Ministry and Bible. For nearly three years, I worked at CrossRoads Church in Lakeville, MN as an intern while playing enough hours of Ultimate Frisbee to receive a Frisbee undergraduate degree.

The summer following graduation, I connected with friends at Sonshine, a Christian Woodstock, and hung out with a guy named Clint Evans. Recognize that last name? Our first date consisted of Applebee's followed by *X-Men II.*

The entire time we dated, I emphasized, "I'm moving home to Chicago as soon as my lease is up. We can't get serious."

Clint and I married one week short of 23 . . . for both of us. He is only four days older than me, I used to say, "I want my husband to be older than me, but not too much older."

After I met Clint I called my sister, Jorie. "His birthday is April 2nd."

"Well, that's older, but not too much older," she replied.

What can I say? The man was persistent.

That, and God has a sense of humor. God and I reached a certain understanding about my life. I tell God what I refuse to do. Then, He laughs at the absurdity of my ultimatums. Despite my incessant protests, I'm always blessed when things happen God's way.

People believe I'm in better standing with God as a youth minister. They don't understand the understanding between God and myself.

I once planned a trip to visit my mom the same week she planned a cross-country motorcycle trip. Communication is not our forte.

When friends cancelled her trip, she said,

"So 'Sman-tha,' I hope you didn't pray for a cancellation." My family morphed my name into two syllables.

"I don't need to pray, Mom. God and I just have an understanding."

My family is pretty tight—even the cousins. I told God, "I'll attend Northwestern as long as I can return to Chicagoland after graduation to be near my family."

I also told God, "I'll never work in a Lutheran church." Their liturgical services weren't my first worship style of choice.

Two years and two thousand miles from home later, I moved to Oregon to work at a Lutheran Church.

Remember those blessings I talked about? All the Lutherans I met were pretty darn nice—and they definitely know how to potluck. I'm convinced potlucks are a cross-denominational talent.

The two things we all share in common? Christ and potlucks. Christian community should really be that simple.

I also told God, "I'll never be a pastor's wife. I don't want that call."

You already know the punch line.

Clint returned home from school one day and said, "God did not call me to be a counselor. God called me to be a pastor."

Thanks for that.

As a good, supportive wife, I replied, "No, I think you're wrong. Try praying again."

Clint. He's a one-word sentence in and of himself. If you knew him you'd understand. Clint was a drug addict and alcoholic before the

legal drinking age. Many 21-year-olds buy their first legal drink: Clint checked himself into Teen Challenge, a Christian rehab facility.

His first week there, God knocked him upside the head with a spiritual-size 2" X 4" to grab Clint's attention. Seven years and a pastor's heart later, he worked at a Teen Challenge addiction recovery center.

The story of the lost son in Luke 15 is Clint's story. He ran away from God, then found his way back again. My husband inscribed tattoos on each forearm, spelling out "Prodigal Son." The face of a lion covers one upper arm. Clint's other arm depicts a lamb.

He shaved his head, bulked up quite a bit, and started playing semi-pro football. He sports a mustache and goatee. He looks more and more like a skinhead. Some sweet, little, old ladies at our church scuttle away from him, which he hates. He doesn't much appreciate police officers shadowing and profiling him, either. Often times, teenagers, and sometimes grown men, who pass him on the street, eye him with trepidation—this, Clint thinks is hysterical.

While words like "strong" and "tough" often describe my husband, his center is mushy.

He'll try to tell you he's an idiot, but don't listen to him—he's an idiot. He's incredibly smart, especially with people.

He reads philosophy books *just for fun*. I told him, "Idiots don't read philosophy books for fun."

He didn't listen—because he's an idiot.

Convinced we'd raise "little line-backers," when we found out we were pregnant, Clint declared,

"My child is going to be a man mountain of awesomeness." That phrase was taken from a commercial featuring Brian Urlacher, a Chicago Bear linebacker. Then Clint added, "even if the baby's a girl."

A startling image hijacked my brain—my precious daughter sporting a full goatee.

I must also add—Clint is a Vikings fan. I asked his brother Darry, "What do you get when you cross a Bears fan with a Vikings fan?"

"I don't know. What?" He asked.

"I don't know," I replied. "I hoped you could tell me. I guess we'll find out in May when our baby arrives."

We didn't find out. That May miscarriage interrupted our lives. Sometimes I feel like my pregnancy didn't really happen.

Do you feel that way, too? Are you out there, feeling what I feel? I know I'm not alone. Common threads weave our miscarriage stories together. So, despite the foreign pain within my chest, I decided to share my story and the stories of other women whom I know.

Why? So you know you're not alone, either.

Let me begin at the beginning: Clint and I agreed in May that I would not refill my prescription for birth control pills at the end of July.

July 3rd was the first day of my last period. Ten days later?

I was pregnant.

From May to August, my insides strained with the effort required to keep our secret. Well, all right, so I told one friend. I needed to tell *someone.*

Reflection: What's On My Heart?

After any traumatic loss, it's normal to wonder: *Where did my identity go?* For now, circle words that best describe you:

above average	callous	crafty	enthusiastic
adventurous	candid	cranky	evasive
affectionate	careful	curious	excitable
agreeable	careless	cynical	fastidious
ambitious	cautious	dainty	ferocious
amiable	charming	decisive	fervent
amusing	cheerful	delightful	fiery
analytical	chic	devoted	flaky
athletic	churlish	diligent	flashy
apathetic	circumspect	direct	frank
apprehensive	civil	discerning	friendly
ardent	clever	discreet	funny
artistic	clumsy	dramatic	fussy
assertive	competent	dutiful	generous
attentive	composed	eager	gentle
balanced	confident	earnest	graceful
beautiful	confused	easy-going	grouchy
blunt	considerate	efficient	guarded
boisterous	content	egotistical	hearty
brave	cool-headed	emotional	helpful
bright	cooperative	encouraging	hot-headed
brilliant	cordial	energetic	hysterical
buff	courageous	enterprising	idiotic

imaginative	old-fashioned	respected	superficial
impatient	orderly	respectful	surly
impetuous	ostentatious	responsible	suspicious
impractical	outgoing	restless	sweet
impulsive	outspoken	sad	tactful
indefatigable	passionate	sassy	tactless
independent	passive	saucy	talented
indiscreet	patient	self-assured	testy
industrious	peaceful	sensible	thinker
insensitive	persevering	sensitive	thoughtful
inspiring	persnickety	sentimental	thoughtless
intelligent	picky	serene	timid
inventive	playful	serious	tolerant
jovial	pleasant	sharp	touchy
joyous	plucky	short-tempered	tranquil
kind	polite	shy	unbalanced
level-headed	positive	silly	uncertain
lively	powerful	sincere	uncooperative
logical	practical	sleepy	undependable
long-winded	prejudiced	sloppy	unflappable
maternal	proficient	slow	unguarded
mature	proud	smart	unsure
methodical	provocative	snazzy	versatile
meticulous	prudent	somber	vigilant
modest	punctual	sophisticated	volcanic
motivated	quick	soulful	vulnerable
musical	quick-tempered	soulless	warm
naive	quiet	spirited	warmhearted
natural	realistic	stable	wary
naughty	reassuring	steady	watchful
nervous	reclusive	stern	weak
noisy	reliable	stoic	well-rounded
nosy	reserved	strong	willing
obliging	resigned	subtle	zealous
obnoxious	resourceful	sulky	zippy

Letter from God to Self

After my miscarriage, I attended a ministry training retreat. Participants were told to write a letter from God to ourselves. Here's what I wrote:

Dear Sam,

I invite you to remember the river where your heart felt utter peace in the midst of calamity. Rest in Who I am. I am mighty. I am moving and I am bringing the Evans with Me. I've got you.

This next part will be hard, but I have built you and Clint to withstand the storm. You do not have to hold onto Me, because I am holding on to you.

There will be freedom that you cannot imagine, fulfillment that you cannot fathom and prosperity beyond your wildest dreams on the other side of this adventure. Te amo. Te amado.

Love, Your Father

"You saw my body as it was formed. All the days planned for me were written in your book before I was one day old," Psalm 139:16, ICB.

Write a letter from God to yourself, if you want. If you can't find the words, no problem.

When the dust of mourning settles, I will find myself again.

Name: **Date:**

3 Pregnancy Excitement

Most pregnancies begin the same way—with, what I like to call "the fun part."

When the birth control left my system, at the beginning of August, my hormones shot through the roof. I often chased my husband down—not that he ever put up a fight.

While on my back, sometimes I thought: *We could be making a baby right now.* Since we got pregnant so fast, sex never felt like a chore to check off a list.

Following the miscarriage, when I mentioned that detail to others they said, "Oh, you'll have no trouble getting pregnant again!"

You can't promise that. Do you really think a new baby will replace the one I lost? Does that unsubstantiated promise help you feel better? Their hollow words failed to comfort or encourage me.

Maybe you struggled to get pregnant. Did you try a year *before* you miscarried, like my late-thirty-something, cousin Jenny? Two years after her miscarriage, Jenny was *still* not pregnant.

My friend Misty miscarried and waited two years before she conceived her first son. Despite

raising three healthy sons, Misty's 30-year-old pregnancy loss still leaves a vivid scar.

Or maybe, your story is like Sandie or Diane's. You experienced multiple miscarriages and still-births. Yet, never felt the slight weight of your own child tucked within your arms. With each loss, grief digs a hole so deep you doubt you can crawl out.

And maybe you're not even sure if you want to conceive a child. Perhaps, pregnancy isn't exciting at all, but terrifying.

I suspected I might be pregnant two weeks after conception. I maintained a six-pack into adulthood. Huge thighs. Fine, scraggly hair. But, picturesque abs.

Following a medium-level abdominal workout in early September my abs felt tender. *Maybe I need to work out more. Maybe I'm just getting older.*

That same morning, I returned home from my run, and my nipples *hurt. Why are my nipples chaffing?*

I stretched my sports bra away from my chest to investigate, then gasped. "'Purple nurples' are *not* a myth."

After a steadying breath I exclaimed, "Well, *that's* not normal."

Over the next few days, I noticed other minute changes. My belly button itched. My fingers recognized the shape of my navel had shifted. Don't deny the truth—you know you stick your fingers in your innie or outie sometimes, too.

The infamous 'pregnant glow' was really just a nice way of saying "oily, and somewhat zitty face."

I coulda sworn under oath, something with

powerful claws pried my abs apart like a zipper.

My friend, Dia, noticed my slick, pimply complexion. "You're glowing. Are you late?"

"Possibly," I replied. "My cycles haven't evened out yet since stopping the pill."

The next day during an adult Bible study at church, I whispered to my friend Emily, "I'm six days late."

"Go take the test!"

"I thought the test only worked with the first pee of the day."

"No." Emily shot me a sideways glance.

"Don't you need to wait a few weeks?"

"No! Take the test and put me out of my misery."

"Pushy."

"Go!" Emily whispered in a stage whisper.

"I can't leave now. I work here. It's Sunday morning."

After skipping a period three years before, I purchased birth control and two pregnancy tests in the same transaction. After church, I rifled around under the bathroom sink until I found that slim, white package.

Clint and I had invited two teen brothers to our home for lunch. While these brothers waited in the living room—oblivious—Clint failed at nonchalance in the kitchen beyond the bathroom.

I peed on the stick and emerged from the bathroom grinning. *Act like an adult. It's totally normal to wave a urine-soaked stick in front of someone's face.*

Clint read my excitement, then his eyes dropped to my plastic-encased body waste.

"We're pregnant?" His face radiated with wonder.

AJ and Nick appeared in the kitchen. "You're pregnant?"

"Which one wants to be the first one to pray for our baby?" Clint asked.

"I will," Nick volunteered.

The three guys placed their hands on my shoulders and we bowed our heads as Nick escorted us into the throne room. Not *that* throne room, but that personal space where we draw near to God's throne of grace in prayer.

> *September 16: Dear Baby Evans, It's just you and me until May. I want to take advantage of our alone time. For these next nine months, I'll share with you my experiences, words shared by others, and my thoughts and prayers. Some details you may wish you could forget. Others, I pray you will always cherish. Here's to us. Here's to the love we'll share with each other. Here's to the LORD, who gave us a wonderful gift in each other. I love you, Sweetheart. —Mom*

These journal entries chronicling a part of my story, recall vivid descriptions that would be more accurate than my memory in years—even months—to come. As I lived with the surreal loss, these entries reminded me that, despite the lack of evidence, my experience really happened.

I was pregnant.

A child grew within me.

I am a mother who lost her child.

I am changed as a person for a reason.

The journal entries written *prior* to discovering

I was pregnant made *way* more sense *after* confirming I was pregnant.

> *August 14: I went for a bike ride today. After only six miles on a semi-hot day, I felt light-headed and thirsty. I couldn't figure out why.*

> *August 20: Went waterskiing and ziplined with teenagers. Earlier today, I shared with Kyle [a colleague] that I couldn't stay focused. I probably just need to settle into the routine of the school year.*

Turns out, there *was* more to the story.

> *August 27: Heard a voice in the back of my head telling me not to give blood. At my insistence, Clint said, "You're being ridiculous." Then he hugged me. "I know you're excited, Baby. We'll get pregnant someday."*

Ha ha. The joke was on us.

I texted a picture of my pregnancy test to *everyone.* Did you not receive your jpeg? One friend screamed and squealed about becoming an auntie, just as I hoped she would. She was an *excellent* first person to tell.

While I spoke on the phone with her, my youngest sister texted, "Is this real? Am I going to be an aunt?"

Many individuals didn't answer right away. Figured.

I called my friend Carolyn twice and left a message once. When she called . . . I answered, "Hey, Care."

"Are you pregnant?"

Good friends require little preamble.

AJ, Nick, and I finally sat at our dining room table to eat pasta. Clint's super-sonic bass voice reverberated through the open windows with the warm, autumn wind as he spoke to his parents.

My dad called me and I answered the phone at the table. "Dad, are you ready to be a Grandpa?"

My middle sister's voice interrupted. "What, Sman-tha, really?"

"Yeah, Dad. I'm pregnant. Hi, Jorie."

"Congratulations!" My dad replied. "Was this planned?"

"Yes," I said, "Look at the text I just sent."

Jorie grabbed the phone. "Sman-tha, Congratulations! So this was planned?" The dialogue worked itself out like a skit . . .

"Yes. We didn't have to wait long. I was only off the pill ten days."

"Wow. That's fast," Jorie said.

"Yeah, Clint has super-sperm."

I forgot, absolutely totally forgot, that two teenage boys sat across the table from me. Nick choked and noodles spewed onto the table.

"Finished eating, Nick?" His older brother mocked.

Oops. I grimaced. "Sorry, Nick."

Later that evening, I texted my cousin, Debi. I was to march down the aisle as a bridesmaid in her March wedding.

"Umm . . . going to be a bit bigger for your wedding."

Excited, Debi phoned and left a five-minute voice mail. Debi speaks in fast forward and her speech was near intelligible. I deciphered from the

300-second message: "Was this planned, or were you just being sneaky. I saw you two months ago. You didn't say a word. This will, of course, go in our book." Debi and I were co-writing *African Grey,* a novel.

I called Debi back. "Planned. We didn't waste time. We've only been trying for ten days. In front of a freshman boy, I joked to Jorie, 'Clint has super sperm.' Poor boy couldn't finish his lunch."

Debi's laughter carried across two time zones.

"Super Sperm" plus Nick and his noodles, transformed into my favorite answer to the most frequently asked question—"Was this planned?"

> *September 7: Your dad and I went on a seven-mile hike at Silver Creek Falls to celebrate. Got a little light-headed once or twice.*

> *September 8: I announced my pregnancy to council. They cheered. Pastor Jeff prayed for you, "That their baby would be full of energy and life—which I don't think will be much of a problem considering your parents."*

> *September 12: I dreamed I gave birth to a banana slug. Never should have looked at the four-week pictures. You look like a big sluggish clump of cells.*

> *September 20: I don't feel pregnant anymore. Haven't for a few days. I told Dia I expected the doctor to say, "Just kidding! You aren't pregnant!" "That's normal," Dia reassured me. "I felt the same way."*

"There is a time to cry

and

a time to laugh.

There is a time to be

sad and

a time to dance

with joy."

Ecclesiastes 3:4,
ERV

September 21: Well, it's official. You're official, I should say. Went to the doctor's office and peed in a cup so they could tell me what I already knew—I'm pregnant. The confirmation relieved an invisible weight from my shoulders. Wow. I'm pregnant. I can't believe it.

Your stories, like mine, are true. They're a part of you. You likely cried about your loss. Have you smiled about the pregnancy? Have you laughed about the announcements? Both sadness and joy share equal importance on this unexpected journey you find yourself on.

Your child wiggled atop your bladder and simultaneously snuggled his or her way into your heart. Take quick inventory of yourself. Is grief threatening to clamp a tourniquet around your vital organs?

I wrote a quote on the inside of a photo album:

> *"Don't cry because it's over. Smile because it happened."*

I'm not there yet. You may not be, either. I pray that one day we'll possess the strength to "smile because the pregnancy happened."

Reflection: What's On My Heart?

Recording the truth of your pregnancy requires courage, effort, and your time. Mom, you owe yourself the truth. Your body changed. Your womb cradled a baby within. You are a mother who lost her child. Grab a pen and a huge box of tissues. I'll meet you on the other side.

Pregnancy: Surprised or planned?

How long it took to get pregnant.

Gender I hoped for.

When I suspected I was pregnant.

Draw your facial expression when you discovered you were pregnant.

How I confirmed my pregnancy.

What changes did I make after becoming pregnant?

Who were the first people I told and what were their reactions?

Details I don't want to forget.

I'm back! As promised, I'm right here. How did your mini-journaling session go? I'm so proud of you for recalling the precious life you carried inside your womb.

In the Words of Others

Dear Parents of Loss,

Our marriage started 13 months after our wedding, because I deployed to Korea two weeks after the ceremony. Other than a month-long furlough, my wife and I didn't see one another for a year.

I returned stateside and within one week, we packed all our belongings and transitioned to my assignment in Texas. A couple weeks later, boxes still unpacked, I came home from work and Julee fished a pregnancy test out of the garbage.

"It was negative," she said, on the verge of tears.

"Aw, sweetheart, I'm sorry." I wrapped my arm around her, glanced at the pregnancy test, and saw two little lines in the window. "Um . . ."

Faster than a patriot missile flies, she went from sad to shocked to tentative to hopeful to ecstatic. She spent the next few hours calling everyone she knew, and some people she didn't. She collected blankets and books and baby paraphernalia I didn't even know existed. "What to Expect When Your Expecting" moved from room to room so often I wondered if the book itself grew legs.

Prenatal visits in the military didn't start until 12 weeks. When my wife started spotting, we experienced a little scare at seven weeks and one day.

"It's called a threatened miscarriage, but the baby is fine," the doctor assured us. "Everything looks normal. We'll see you back in five weeks."

At our first official prenatal visit, the technician performed the ultrasound. "All right. Let me grab the doctor."

"Our first baby . . . " Julee chatted excitedly. I don't remember a word she said. She wasn't facing the monitor, but I was. The baby had no heartbeat.

The doctor performed another ultrasound, then told us the baby died at seven weeks and two days.

The thought boggled my mind that her body rejected the pregnancy, but retained the baby as if Julee herself willed the baby to remain cradled within her.

We're so sorry for your loss. We know how you feel.

Your friends,

Tom and Julee

4 Celebrate Your Baby's Life

Losing my baby's life caused me to value life. I cherish each moment I shared with my child. My journal entries—and this book—celebrate life.

The words of Psalms 139: 13–14, NIV leapt off the page as the Psalmist declared:

> *"For you created my inmost being. You knit me together in my mother's womb. I praise you because I am fearfully and wonderfully made. Your works are wonderful; I know that full well."*

The miracle of my pregnancy was wonderful—at first. As God wove my child together in my womb, I . . .

- thought about every food morsel that entered my mouth in a whole new way
- wondered how every activity in which I participated affected my baby
- cared for my child when my baby could give me absolutely nothing in return.

Just his or her presence, inside of me, growing, safe and protected . . . was enough. I made changes in my eating and activities to protect my child. Did you?

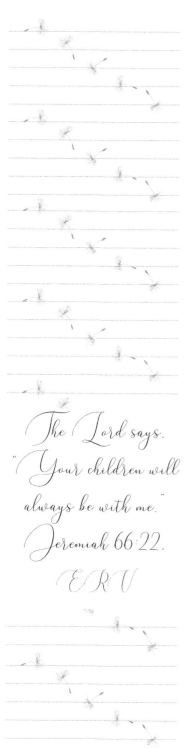

The Lord says, "Your children will always be with me."

Jeremiah 66:22.

ERV

Now that we've lost our babies, you and I feel real pain—raw, knock-the-wind-out-of-us, earth-shattering pain. Our loss is real, because our children existed.

More than 20 years later, Aunt Mary still misses her babies. "Every November, I'm sad." She chuckled about a memory. "On the one-year birthday, a good friend brought me balloons to celebrate."

Aunt Mary never exchanged a first glance with her stillborn baby. To treasure her child's life—a real life—she held a graveside memorial service. She recalled a memory, "My daughters were old enough to place flowers on the baby's casket."

I stifled a gasp. She buried her baby. *How difficult. How precious. How healing.*

Aunt Mary's second miscarriage was a year before the birth of her youngest child, Robert.

Even if others struggle to comprehend this reality, our children were real. On All Saints Day "Baby Evans" was included in the names of our church members who passed away that year. To honor the life of my child, I considered donating flowers to the church on the Sunday closest to the due date.

Remember your child. How have you celebrated your baby? Have you journaled your story? Drawn pictures? Held a memorial service? How you remember your child is personal and can take many forms. Below are ways other moms honored and remembered their babies:

- name your child
- adopt a pet from a shelter or rescue group
- eat cake on your baby's birthday due date

- give a contribution in your child's name to a local or favorite charitable organization
- hang a Christmas ornament on the tree
- insert flowers or a message in a bottle and cast it in a stream, a river, or the ocean
- journal or blog about your feelings about being pregnant, how you felt about the loss, and how you coped each day
- light a candle during a holiday dinner
- make or buy a keepsake charm or custom piece of jewelry to remember your baby
- name a star after your angel baby
- paint or buy a piece of art that expresses your love for your child
- place your positive pregnancy test, cards, sonograms, pressed flowers, and other mementos in a memory box
- place the picture of the first pregnancy test in your wallet or on your fridge
- plant a tree, a rosebush, or a favorite flower
- sponsor a child in poverty at home or around the world whose birthday shares your child's due date
- start or participate in a miscarriage support group
- write a letter or poem to your baby.

Remember your child. Your child wasn't 'just' a fetus or a clump of cells. Cherish your baby's life —and your life. The greatest way to honor your child? Keep on living.

As if God foreshadowed the loss, some entries in my journal carried a prophetic air.

September 20: I don't really feel pregnant anymore. Haven't for a few

"I received a small heart from a friend I could hold in my pocket and a tiny little ring from the hospital. When I felt better, I passed them forward to a couple friends who miscarried. They still use them."

Bridget,
Minnesota

1st Edition Reader

Great gift ideas include a memorial necklace, bracelet, or an ornament."

Amy, California.

Member of the Love Letters to Miscarriage moms Facebook Page

days. I told Dia that I was scared that I was going to go to the doctor and they'd tell me I was wrong. She reassured me that that was normal; told me she'd felt the same way with Nada and Maleana. I guess it's normal for pregnant women to have CRAZY dreams too. September 12th I dreamed that I was giving birth to a banana slug. Never should have looked at the four-week pictures. You looked like a big sluggish clump of cells.

Everyone has been asking me if I've gotten sick. When I say "No," they stare at me in awe, so thank you for that.

Celebrate your child's life. Memorialize your child, however you know how. Will it hurt? Heck, yeah. If we make the most of our children's brief lives and cherish the time we shared together, then maybe in the future, we'll remember our babies, members of our family, with fondness and joy.

Reflection: What's On My Heart?

Name Your Child

In the heart below write a message to your child or:

- the name you wanted for a boy
- the name you wanted for a girl.

How do I want to celebrate my child's life?

Who will I ask to help me memorialize my child?

In the Words of Others

Dear Mom,

One year I dropped two gold feathers in a clear Christmas ornament and gifted it to my sister, who lost two babies. Each year she hangs the ornament on her Christmas tree to reflect on those babies.

I hang an ornament on my tree as well. Each year I add a new feather to the ornament to honor and celebrate each year of my baby's life in heaven.

Taylor

Florida

5 Delivering the Miscarriage Announcement

I stared at my pale reflection in the dresser mirror with the phone pressed against my cheek. "Emily, I've told *so many* people we're pregnant. We already posted on Facebook! Now I'm obligated to announce to a gazillion people we're *not* pregnant anymore. 'Ha ha. Just kidding.'"

Many friends warned us to wait 8-12 weeks prior to announcing our pregnancy. But Emily advised, "Sam, I don't agree with waiting until the second trimester to tell people. If something *does* happen, you'll want people to know."

As we spoke about my loss, she reiterated the same truth. "The last thing you need to worry about right now is announcing your miscarriage to everyone. Don't worry about them. Worry about you."

While Emily's words helped, they failed to ease the embarrassment haunting me.

"I have no idea how moms-to-be keep the 'I'm pregnant' secret for so long," I remarked to Clint following our miscarriage. "Now I wish we'd waited. I'm so ashamed." Somehow I also felt

like I disappointed my extended family who were so excited!

Clint smiled and kissed my bedhead hair. "No, Sweetie, you were *so* happy."

I was euphoric. On September 6, 2009, I posted on Facebook:

> "Gonna be a mom this Mother's Day.

Every few minutes I checked my post to see how many more people congratulated me.

I also texted a picture of the pregnancy test to several close friends because—in my elated brain—that felt normal. So possibly the most disturbing Facebook comment was:

> Oh yeah, D just got the pic on his phone to show, LOL.

Show to whom?

At that time, I was too happy to care. *Forward the photo to the whole world!*

Until my turn to experience miscarriage arrived, I didn't realize how left out I felt not being a parent. Three weeks following my pregnancy post, the baby was gone.

How do you announce to a fertile world? "I'm no longer pregnant."

A week after the miscarriage—one month after my "I'm pregnant" post, I worked up the gumption to share my hard truth on Facebook.

October 6, 2009:

> Okay. I'm ready to say this. I miscarried on Sept 27th. It's been a really sucky week. Today is going to be a hard day. I can feel it.

From my "I confess I miscarried" social media announcement, here's the most important take-away: I zoomed in on the embarrassment, leaving no room to imagine the outpouring of love from my friends and family. My people encouraged me.

Lots of prayers coming your way.

Love you, Sweetie.

Sam, just saw your post. I am truly sorry for your loss. Hang in there, kid.

Sam I am so terribly sorry. My thoughts and prayers are with you in this time of sadness and heartache.

My people publicly shared their hard truths with me.

I've been there, twice, before I had my girls.

Sorry to hear the news. Keep in mind something like 1 in 4 pregnancies end in miscarriage. I had a miscarriage, too before I got pregnant with Christopher.

A teenage boy from my youth group (miracles do happen) wrote:

Sam that is truly saddening to hear. Please know that my and my family's prayers are with you. And don't give up. There's a reason for the six-year split with me and Ryan, God will reward your faith beyond any misery.

One friend actually made me laugh.

Sam my friend, that is a low down, dirty, heartbreaking shame. If I find any good vibes lying around I will send them immediately.

A friend loves you all the time, but a brother was born to help in times of trouble.
Proverbs 17:17. ERV

So, share when you want and how you want. Just know this, when you do, your friends will love you through your heartache.

If you're too devastated to tell others or prefer to avoid dealing with other people's responses, ask someone close to you—a friend, family member, or co-worker—to break the news.

Or get creative. One friend, a minister's wife, miscarried in Canada, a day after arriving at her in-laws' home.

When she returned to the States, she didn't understand her feelings. Embarrassed, she didn't want to talk about her miscarriage with anyone in their church. She made the deliberate decision to phone the church's gabbiest gossiper to tell her every gory detail.

Gossip spread the story. The minister's wife never needed to say a word to anyone, or answer any inappropriate questions from nosy church members.

Three months later, after the doctor told her husband not to wear tight underwear, because heat kills sperm, ta-da—she was pregnant! Thirty years later, she still giggles about telling the church gossip.

Hot Tip #1

Ask for help to break the news. Call two or three key people. Decide on the instructions you want them to communicate to your extended family and friends.

I want to be contacted by:

- a call
- a text

- an email
- a letter or card
- or not at all.

Regarding books (with the exception of this amazing *Love Letters to Miscarriage Moms*):

- Send them my way, because I need all the help I can get
- Sure, send them, because I'm out of kindling
- If I receive any more books, I may lose my fragile grip on my sanity.

Hot Tip #2: (Refer to Hot Tip #1)

This personal time of grief is yours. The choice to answer or ignore a call, text, email, or letter is your decision. Don't feel guilty about utilizing caller ID. If you don't feel like talking—don't. Your friends will understand.

Your needs may startle you if they are different since the miscarriage. Listen to yourself.

Jenny said, "Really hard things that happen to people change who they are. This grief is a really personal journey."

I can't prescribe how best for you to proceed. If you want to announce and/or talk about how you feel about your loss on Facebook or your blog, you know yourself best. If you prefer not to tell others, that's your choice, also.

No two women experience the same circumstances regarding how they conceived their child. No two women share the same particulars surrounding their pregnancy. Getting pregnant means something different to each woman. I'll wager

you have witty stories about your pregnancy discovery.

Don't be afraid to laugh at the memories. Don't be afraid to make room for the baby in your heart the way your body made room right smack on top of your bladder. Your body and emotions changed because your womb cradled a baby within.

You're a mother who lost her child. No matter how long the pregnancy lasted, every miscarriage mother processes her mourning in her own way and on her own timeline. This fact remains—we bonded with our babies, who were real.

I encourage you to share your story with those you trust. Some miscarriage moms find comfort and support in sharing their feelings. If you're a talker, like me, this presents no challenge.

Or, are you a private person who finds expressing your feelings too painful? Is telling others you lost your child too difficult? You may feel more comfortable finding a miscarriage support group in a closed, online community.

Own your story. Give yourself time to remember the joy or the shock of discovering you were pregnant. Allow yourself time to mourn your loss.

Don't allow anyone to pressure you into sharing your story a certain way. The ifs, whens, and hows of talking about your pregnancy loss with others is totally up to you.

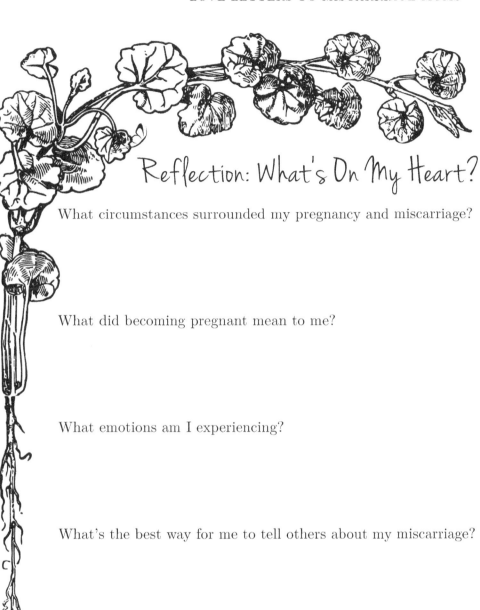

Reflection: What's On My Heart?

What circumstances surrounded my pregnancy and miscarriage?

What did becoming pregnant mean to me?

What emotions am I experiencing?

What's the best way for me to tell others about my miscarriage?

List the key people who will break the news. What instructions do I want them to tell extended family and friends?

In the Words of Others

Dear Mom,

This was my public miscarriage announcement.

There is a unique pain that comes from preparing a place in your heart for a child that never comes. August 26th was supposed to be a special day for us.

We'd only been married a few months, and everyone around us said: "Don't have kids."

"Wait."

"Take time for just the two of you."

Then we found out we were pregnant. At first I was shocked, and honestly a little upset, but dismay soon turned into excitement. I had my first appointment and everything was perfect.

Fast forward two weeks—everything changed.

Miscarriage.

I never imagined miscarriage would happen to me. We were very private about our loss and didn't really tell anyone. Why is miscarriage such a silent torture? Why doesn't anyone talk about it?

Suddenly, everyone around me was pregnant. Pregnant moms honestly still bother me. It's so hard.

Everyone wants to say they know how you feel, and they know what it's like, but they don't. No one understands until they experience a miscarriage. I will never know the reason why this happened to us. But I do know that God's plan is always so much greater than ours.

#imtiredofthesilence #miscarriage #iam1in4

Love, Danielle

6 The No Good, Bad, Most Terrible Day

SPOILER ALERT: *Compounded by the mental, emotional anguish and turmoil of losing a life, the physical aspects of miscarriage can be horrific and grotesque to some. The following was written to validate the pain of a miscarriage survivor. If you prefer to skip the following graphic scene regarding the blood loss of miscarriage turn to page 52. You've been warned.*

> *September 28: I'm not pregnant anymore . . . Brown spotting turned into pink into red . . . darker red to thicker.*

The spotting began during church Sunday morning and continued throughout the day. Trying not to worry about the blood, I placed a pad in my underwear.

Sometimes pregnant women spot, right? This is normal. This might be normal.

Hope waned as daylight faded into twilight. Forced to pretend I was fine, I led youth group while the inner workings of my body plagued me. That evening, Clint and I cozied down to watch

a movie. Dull cramps pounded like a sledge hammer to the belly. Our cat, my fluffy, gray heating pad, leapt off my lap. Two friends offered futile attempts to alleviate my fear.

"Don't worry yet, Sam. Some women spot."

The other friend said, "You'd know if you were miscarrying. Miscarriage cramps feel 10 times worse than PMS cramps."

"You didn't know me in high school," I replied. "I had a reserved cot in the nurse's office each month."

I remember one nurse yelling, "Why don't you take something for the pain!"

I might have retorted if I could see straight. Clearly, she never experienced cramps as intense as mine. While some cars accelerate from 0–60 MPH in seconds, my cramps shot from zero-zilch to full-blown-turn-your-uterus-inside-out-cramps within minutes. If I arrived home from high school before my sisters, or they noticed my backpack dumped in the foyer, they knew not to say a word to the sleeping bear upstairs.

Despite the visceral memory of PMS prior to starting the pill—an invention for which God deserves my deepest heartfelt gratitude—my friends' words gave me pause. *Maybe I'm not miscarrying after all.*

That Sunday night, however, I learned that miscarriage cramps felt no different than the ones I experienced throughout high school and college.

September 28: My cramps propelled me into the bathtub. The hot water assuaged the pain. Just when I thought I exaggerated my fears, I

It's 3 a.m.. I wish the sky would burst with rain. I would so turn on Matchbox 20 right now. I'm so tired.

Sam.

queefed and passed a quarter-sized clump of bloody tissue. I picked up the bloody glob, staring at it in my hand.

I don't know how many mothers who miscarry are granted the same opportunity. I wish they all did. Closure.

Head, lighter in shade, arms and legs of the thumbnail-sized baby tucked together in a fetal position, I gazed at him or her—so anxious for life, he came out eight months too soon. Fascinated by a wonder glimpsed by very few people, I held my baby. I touched my whole child with the tip of my finger. My child, mine and Clint's, whom God formed inside of me.

I wear the purity ring from my father on my right hand, to set an example for the teens in my youth group. The phrase "True Love Waits" acquired a brand new meaning as I stared.

"Cli . . ." no sound accompanied my attempt to speak. "Clint!" My shouted word exited as a whisper. One more try.

"Clint!"

He sprinted to the bathroom and ripped back the shower curtain. I lifted my hand and showed him our miracle.

To this day he wishes I hadn't.

10-year hindsight:

I wish

I'd buried him in the backyard and planted flowers.

Instead.

I never received

the baby back.

the test cost $300.00

and revealed nothing

I am

I handed the baby to Clint. He placed the baby in a plastic bag and set him in the fridge. Maybe the doctor could give us a reason.

I drained the red bathwater and showered the blood off my skin.

My stomach waved with an involuntary, cartoon-esque motion.

"Woah. What?" Amazement vanished when I felt a hard contraction and a 16-inch-softball-size clump of tissue splattered onto the bathtub floor. The forming placenta. Another glob of tissue followed.

It's 3 a.m., I wish the sky would burst with rain. I would so turn on Matchbox 20 right now. I'm so tired.

Before bed I used the bathroom four times, each time discharging smaller amounts of blood. I expelled so much blood in 15 hours.

I'd kicked the clumps down the drain in tears. "All r-right, all r-right," I screamed. "I get it! I'm not pregnant anymore!"

That's when reality hit. For three weeks I grinned like an idiot, exclaiming to everyone—family, friends, even cashiers in checkout lines, "I'm pregnant!"

Now I clutched my stomach. Tears flowed with as much force of the shower stream and merged, trickling down the drain. "I'm not pregnant anymore!"

Unbeknownst to me, Clint sat stockstill in the bathroom just beyond the tub, oblivious to the world beyond the cocoon we created in that small room. Some part of him died that day too. The loss of his baby carved a piece from his heart, leaving a void in its place.

"Yes! What the hell does that mean?" My shout jerked Clint out of his trance.

"Sam, are you talking to me?"

"What? No. Oh . . . You're in here?" Obviously. "Never mind. No, I was talking to God." Later that night as I journaled I wrote these words:

> *You see . . . in the middle of my crying God caught me off guard with the most absurd question: "Are you ready to be blessed now?"*
>
> *That's how I know I heard God—because God is crazy and rarely ever makes sense. Anger trumped response.*
>
> *God repeated. He doesn't like being ignored, "Are you ready to be blessed?"*
>
> *"Yes!" These are the words Clint heard, while I showered, "But what the hell does that mean?"*
>
> *I don't usually answer God out loud, but God's posed question rang out nearly audibly. Speaking out loud also drew me closer to Him and I needed God to feel real.*

That "you see" epiphany became a pivotal moment in my writing.

That's when I began writing for you.

Man . . . God is so sneaky.

I whimpered, "More blood?" as I watched it swirl down the drain. "There's so much blood."

"Sam, please let me take you to the ER," Clint pleaded.

"No. I'm fine."

Maybe you're reading this and wondering, like my poor husband, why I didn't let him drive me to the hospital—if you're not already wondering why you chose to read this chapter.

I warned you.

My body cleaned itself out. I planned to call the doctor's office first thing Monday morning. So why go to the ER? As for my abdominal cramps and period-quantity bleeding? That could wait until tomorrow's doctor's visit. I know some pretty great doctors, but I've never met one who could reverse death.

After my shower, the intensity of my sobbing dropped me to my knees. A pad soaked in the lighter bleeding. Like sneezes of the vagina, the toilet caught the thicker blood.

Later, I heard horror stories about women, who unaware of their miscarriages and dead tissue within their bodies, faced a life-threatening infection.

Amidst my intense loss, a stray thought of a peaceful death momentarily appealed to me.

> *Right now, I'm just going to fall asleep next to Clint, for the second time tonight. He fell asleep with his ESPN magazine upright in his hands. Good night, world. I'll see you again tomorrow.*

I remember writing "good night, world, I'll see you tomorrow," as if to assure myself—and you—that I would die by commit suicide. I had too much to live for, despite knowing I'd never be the same.

Looking back, I'm grateful for these things.

I'm grateful the loss happened quickly. From the time the bleeding began until the time I expelled the largest clump of blood, only twelve hours passed.

I'm grateful that not only was I at home, but also in my bathtub, the easiest place to rinse away the mess.

I'm grateful I saw our baby.

I'm grateful for Clint beside me.

I don't know the details of your miscarriage. However, perhaps we share this in common: The thing I'm most grateful for with the miscarriage? It's over.

Even though at the time, I had no idea what God meant, I'm also grateful for these words, "Are you ready to be blessed now?"

Give the Lord a chance to show you how good he is. Great blessings belong to those who depend on him!

Psalm 34:8.
ERV

Reflection: What's On My Heart?

The no good, bad, most terrible day will always snag our memories. Sorrow threatens to swallow us whole. Keep fighting. Stay positive. Do your best. Fight to find your smile again.

You may not feel comfortable talking about your "No Good, Bad, Most Terrible Day" to others. However, a journal provides a safe place to release the internal dialogue rumbling around in your mind. To process the horror, the pain, and the blood, write what you're thinking and feeling to help you process the trauma.

In the Words of Others

Beloved sister,

Don't let the darkness consume you.

I know how easy it can be in this moment to give in to the pain, to be overwhelmed by the grief and the ache in your soul. If you, like me, have battled the demons of depression in your past, this moment might be allowing those demons back in, surrounding you, clamoring at your very life.

Stomp them. Kick them. Slam the door in their face. Do not give in to them.

Your pain and grief is enough in itself. This moment and the days and weeks of sorrow are enough in themselves. The depression, an insidious specter, will try its best to weave its way back into your soul. Don't let the gloom in.

Beloved one, I ache with you. The days after my miscarriage have fuzzy edges, details blurred by the heartbreaking pain of deepest sorrows.

I was aware of the darkness that crept in through the cracks, the darkness I have spent so much of my life battling to keep at bay. I was raw and tender. The sense of slipping away into the bleakness consumed me. The emptiness of my womb matched the empty feelings of my soul.

Only by the grace of God, and the love and support of those I leaned on kept my eyes on the pinprick point of light that I could still see. And I clung as tightly as I could to that light, to hope.

My prayer for you in this moment is that you will be surrounded by ones who love you deeply, who help you carry this heavy burden.

Let them help you carry the burden of mourning.

Sometimes the hardest act is releasing our burdens to another, to allow them to hold the weight of it all. Even if it feels strange and uncomfortable, you're strong enough to accept the love and care of others.

Beloved one, you are a warrior. You are a mother. You will win this day.

From deepest despair to the brightest morning, I am yours.

Stef

Kentucky

7 Post-miscarriage Doctor Visit

Monday morning the sun streamed through the windows as I dressed to head to the hospital. The Three Sisters volcanic mountain peaks towered above the timberline. I glanced at the clock on the wall, measuring the time before my appointment.

Do I have time? Yes.

I reached for my phone and dialed friends, who spoke assurances to me the prior evening. One after the other, I delivered the news: "Our worst fears came true. Everything was not okay. I miscarried."

I called one more person.

"Val. I lost the baby."

"Are you sure?"

"Absolutely."

"Oh, Sam, I'm so sorry . . . "

Then whatever words she spoke dissipated like smoke. At that moment, a schism occurred for me between mothers who experienced miscarriage and mothers who hadn't. Us versus them. My heart throbbed with acute pain.

"Val, hey. I need to let you go. I have a doctor's appointment soon."

Clint drove me to the clinic and I checked in.

A nurse escorted us beyond the waiting room to the examination room. Unaware of life beyond my peripheral, I floated from place to place.

Was last night just a vivid nightmare?

I climbed atop the exam table and shifted. The wax paper crinkled beneath me and echoed off tiny walls that contracted with each minute ticking away.

Finally, the door handle dipped and Dr. Mary entered. I blinked back tears as I explained the particulars of what transpired the night before.

"You had a miscarriage." Her confirmation added another layer of reality.

I miscarried. I was going to have a baby. Now he's gone.

In the weeks that followed, I spoke with my tribe of miscarriage moms to inquire about their hospital visits. For some, the doctor appointment became a catalyst for hope and peace. Most, though, replied that their clinic visits only exacerbated their open wounds. More often than not, their stories reflected jarring experiences.

"Ugh! My doctor was such a butthead!" Erica exclaimed.

On the pill, she checked in with her doctor for abnormal spotting. Pregnancy was the furthest thing from Erica's mind.

"You were pregnant." The doctor's cool, detached words knocked the wind out of Erica. In the same breath, she learned about her pregnancy and her loss.

When Diane arrived at the hospital the orderly/intake nurse behind the counter preoccupied herself with paperwork rather than the blood dripping down Diane's leg.

Recalling the anger toward the nurse, she said, "I'm bleeding all over the place and you want my friggin' insurance? You know, we've got bigger problems here, lady."

Later the nurse attempted to placate her by saying, "Oh, you can have another baby."

Diane never did. She experienced another miscarriage followed by a stillbirth and never carried a child to full term.

I share the following story about my grandmother with the most endearing heart. As Grandma spoke, one thought wandered to another. Multiple times she sidetracked from the purpose of my call. I chuckled to myself. *Focus, Grandma.*

Each of Grandma's miscarriages occurred two or three months into the pregnancy. Despite her 85 years of age and scores of years since her miscarriages, she spoke with vivid recollection.

"My doctor, a big guy, breathed heavily when he arrived after rushing up the steps to see me. His urgency meant a lot: It meant he cared." More than 60 years later she still remembered that specific detail.

Losing a child is devastating. The pain?

Unbearable.

People who haven't experienced a miscarriage just—don't—know. My miscarriage performed a D&C on my heart.

Outsiders are not intentionally insensitive or rude and most say things they hope will help. However, they cannot comprehend the depth of our grief. Like a sharp blade turning in an open wound, their calloused-to-me comments intensified my pain.

Most of us endured the same medical follow-ups

for a child no longer in our womb . . . and that *sucks.* Two weeks after I peed in a cup at the doctor's office to confirm *I was pregnant,* the lab technician drew my blood to measure my hCG levels to confirm *I was no longer pregnant.* In case you experienced a really crummy doctor's visit, erase yours and embrace mine.

After I described my horrific day prior, my doctor encouraged me, "I think you'd be surprised at the number of women who miscarry." She raised her hand, which shocked me.

Doctors can miscarry? Dumb thought, I know. I asked, "Have *you* had a miscarriage?"

"Yes. My first pregnancy, like you."

I already knew she had three young children. "Did you experience any problems after that?"

"No."

I shouldn't have felt grateful for her loss, but her admission comforted me. Not only was my doctor a savvy expert about the physical challenges, her experience with the loss of her firstborn meant she also understood my emotional pain, too.

She explained, "One out of four pregnancies ends in miscarriage. Most, by far, happen in the first trimester."

"Why is that?"

"Up until 11 or 12 weeks the baby is still forming, developing. So, if something's wrong with the DNA, the wrong number of chromosomes, or something's off with meiosis or mitosis (division of cells). You know about that, right?"

"Yeah."

"That causes problems sooner, rather than later."

"What's the percentage of miscarriages *after* the first trimester?"

"I'd say one in a thousand."

"Why does the percentage go down so much?"

"At 12 weeks, sometimes if you're lucky at 11, you hear the baby's heartbeat. At that point the already fully developed baby continues to grow."

"Does my miscarriage make me more susceptible to them in the future?"

"Not at all. I wouldn't start worrying until the third miscarriage."

Another miscarriage? I hadn't considered that possibility. My heart dropped into my stomach. *I won't survive another loss. What if I can't carry a child to full term?*

When I shared this fear with Aunt Mary, she said, "Those are just fears you need to leave with the Lord. The outcome of pregnancy is beyond your control."

I heard the wisdom in her words, yet I held back on handing my fear to God.

He did a bang-up job with this pregnancy. I think I'll pass, thank you.

God still existed, but at that moment, I wasn't too happy with Him.

How did *your* doctor's visit play out? Did you feel encouraged? Hopeless?

Many miscarrying moms face the painful decision, whether to agree to a D&C or not. And many don't even know what this gynecological procedure is. My doctor never mentioned the acronym D&C to me.

When people asked me, "Did you require a D&C?"

Honestly? I didn't even understand what they were referring too. Embarrassment prevented me from asking, "What are you talking about?" Instead, I responded "Um . . . no."

I don't think so? I returned home and googled "DNC." The computer outsmarted my mourning brain by inquiring, "Did you mean D&C?"

Eye roll.

I make no claims to be an expert. From what I researched and what Dr. Google taught me, about half of miscarriages that occur before ten weeks happen naturally. Considered a minor surgery, the necessity of a D&C becomes more likely after the first ten weeks. Mothers with babies who die in utero at four to five months are induced in the Labor and Delivery wing. A D&C follows the induction.

During a pregnancy, the placenta emits the hormone human chorionic gonadotropin (hCG). After a miscarriage, elevated hCG levels indicate the body did not expel all the pregnancy-related tissue. To prevent hemorrhaging and/or infection, a D&C stops the bleeding and removes small pieces of placenta, which can turn septic.

Babies don't necessarily come out in one piece, either. As Diane so 'delicately' explained a D&C, "They basically vacuum the baby out."

When I began processing my experience, I craved camaraderie from other miscarriage moms. Because I saw my baby, I asked other moms, "Did you hold your baby too?" Mothers who endure a D&C don't have that option.

Had I known about D&Cs, I'd have asked my next questions more gently: "How did you react? What did you think? How did you recover?"

If a D&C surgery was performed on you, I'm *so* sorry. Oh, love, I'm so, so sorry.

Lona describes how you may of felt. "Misfortune pointed its finger at me and mocked me."

She laid in a delivery room. Posters on the wall advertised nursing tips, the benefits of breast milk, and SIDS prevention. Down the hall, newborn babies wailed in protest at the harsh transition from the warm, dark uterine cradle to cold air and fluorescent lights.

Lona's hand traveled to her swollen belly. Tears slipped down her cheeks. *That should have been me in just four more months.*

When the hearts of Lona's twins' stopped in utero, a nurse pricked Lona's arm inside her elbow and emptied a syringe of Pitocin into the spongy, clear tube. Contractions started soon after.

When Lona reached 10 centimeters, the doctor entered the room. One by one, Lona delivered each of her heaven-born children.

Was this your experience? Or maybe I'm freaking you out because you *might* need a D&C. Nothing about a miscarriage is clean, or neat, or heart-warming.

D&C's, an unfortunate reality, are a necessary procedure—or evil. More than one woman I interviewed described a D&C as a mandatory abortion for a child she wanted to keep.

Others advised, if you need a D&C, request anesthesia so you're unconscious for the surgery. One does not want to remain awake for the procedure.

If you've had a D&C, I want to offer you a unique opportunity. As an author, I frequently weave fictional stories. Allow me to reframe your

The God of
all comfort

comforts us every time

we have trouble

so that when others

have trouble,

we can comfort them

with the same comfort

God gives us.

2 Corinthians
1:3b-4.
ERV

experience. Own this story and know that you are not alone. You are heard, understood, and loved.

You lie on the hospital bed, shivering in the flimsy, collarless hospital gown tied in the back, exposing your helplessness. Tears that flowed nonstop for days dampen your reddened cheeks.

Fear, desperation, and longing consume you.

Two doctors enter, one male, one female. Sympathy softens their features.

"Are you cold?" He asks.

The female doctor reaches for your favorite hoodie on the chair beside the bed. "Would you like to wear this?" She adjusts the line from the IV, then threads your arms through the sleeves of the sweatshirt.

Warmth. Security.

You inhale a deep breath.

On the wall, behind the male doctor, you spot a framed print of a tropical horizon at sunset.

"Your baby is in heaven already," he says. "Now we need to protect you."

The female doctor grasps your hands. "You're not alone."

A nurse enters and places a seal over your nose and mouth. "You'll be asleep momentarily. When you wake up, there will be no more baby."

Your eyes widen with panic.

"Already in heaven," the male doctor reminds you. "Safe, warm, happy. Your journey is longer, but you'll find your strength again." The last words you hear before you fade into the darkness of deep sleep, "And you will see your child again one day."

I believed my post-miscarriage doctor's visit went as well as possible, considering the circumstances.

Before leaving for home, my doctor warned, then issued these instructions. "You'll continue bleeding for at least a week. No sex for a week or two until you stop bleeding. Do not have unprotected sex until you've experienced at least one normal cycle."

Sex? No thank you. That's what got us into this mess to begin with. I may never want sex again. Sex will just remind me that I'm not pregnant anymore. What if I get pregnant again? What if I never get pregnant again?

The doctor's voice dragged me back to my present reality. "You did not cause the miscarriage—not with exercise, nor anything you ate or drank, nor by having sex. This was not caused by anything *you* did." Then she added. "Doctors could not have stopped it."

Despite my shaking disposition, I left my doctor's office grateful for the visit. As the clinic doors eased closed behind me and I stepped into the sunlight, my heart filled with an inexplicable hope.

For the five days following my miscarriage, my sex drive remained null and void. Even Clint made suggestive remarks about his lack of sex drive. I didn't think waiting would be a problem.

The thought of sex terrified me. I need not have worried. After a few days, my hormones trumped my fear and the doctor's warnings.

Reflection: What's On My Heart?

Find a quiet place. Breathe in a few deep breaths, then journal your thoughts or feelings.

If your post-miscarriage hospital visit exacerbated your open wound, what words of comfort would you offer to someone whose experience was handled with insensitivity?

Reflecting upon those who understood, loved, and supported you, list things you feel grateful for . . .

If a doctor performed a D&C on you, describe a best-case scenario in the space below. Infuse your story with joy and laughter.

Who's in the room with you?

Choose your scene. Are you on a beach? In the mountains?

What do you hear? Taste? Smell? Feel?

In the Words of Others

To: You
From: A 'Been There' Doctor
Subject: The card or letter I wish we all received from our clinics or hospitals

Dear [Insert Name],

As a follow up to our office visit yesterday, I want you to know that we are available for any needs you have by phone and office visit. I am deeply sorry for your loss.

You may have more questions now or sometime in the future. As a mother who has lost a pregnancy, I am especially sensitive to doctor visits and I know how to navigate the medical system.

You may be experiencing physical changes that you would like to talk about. Perhaps you are experiencing feelings that are difficult to sort out. Please know that all of us in the Women's Clinic are here to help you. We can personally relate to the difficulty of "What is the next step after a pregnancy loss?" We also have several partners in the community who can provide expert assistance. I've included several resources with this letter.

Let me know how you are. I also look forward to seeing you at our scheduled clinic visit next week. If you prefer to come in for a visit sooner or talk over the phone, please call 777-777-7777. We have on-call professionals 24/7 during evenings and weekends to provide the attention you need and deserve.

With Sympathy,

Gwenn Garmon

Gwenn Garmon, MS, MD
Wyoming
Women's Health Clinic
777-777-7777

8 Sucker Punches

If you ever want to kill a conversation, introduce miscarriage.

Writers pouring words onto a page enter into a different dimension as they type. The world beyond the computer screen fades into oblivion. That was me when a sharp rapping jerked me out of the rabbit hole.

My heart lurched. One reality replaced the other. Knocking. I rose from my chair as my beats-per-minute slowed back down to normal and I opened the front door.

Two Latter Day Saints men wearing their signature white shirts and ties stood on my porch. "How are you?"

Half my brain remained lost in my work—this book. Their question required several seconds to coalesce. *How am I? Oh.*

I ran my hand across my stiff, greasy hair. *When was the last time I showered? I must look like a crazy cat lady without the cats. What did they ask me? How am I? Right.*

I debated, then opted for the truth, too exhausted and foggy for less. "Not so well, actually. I just miscarried and I'm writing my story. To be honest, I don't really feel like talking right now. But thank you so much for stopping by."

One thing that irles me when tragedy happens—

when someone dies or something—and someone says, "Well, I guess that's God's will," that's bad theology. What a hurtful thing to say to someone. I do not believe God takes people from us. We live in a cursed world and bad things happen."

Clint Evans

At the word miscarriage one young man dropped his head, then said, "Is there anything we can do for you?"

I lifted my eyebrows in surprise. Mad props for the quick recovery.

"Could you pray for me as you walk to the next house? My own prayers are unintelligible at the moment."

Most people who asked how I was doing were not as willing to linger on the topic.

Diane said, "People try to say the right things—"

I interrupted, "but their words fall so short. . . ."

She finished, "because there's nothing anyone can say."

Prior to my miscarriage, I can only recall people saying, "Oh, so-and-so had a miscarriage." Frowny face.

"Oh! That's too bad. I think so-and-so did, too."

"Oh, sad."

"Sad!"

End conversation, new topic.

Before experiencing pregnancy loss, miscarriage happened to someone else—not me—not you. The few times people mentioned their miscarriages I responded in kind. "Oh, that's too bad."

Never, ever could I fathom the weighted meaning of those words—a mother lost her child. Our cultural colloquialism is, "Mommy-to-be," "Daddy-to-be." The presumption that parents become parents on their child's birthday is inaccurate. Miscarriage revealed this truth: We are moms and dads from the moment of conception. Prior to this new reality of loss, I. Could. Not. Fathom.

"After my miscarriage, I didn't want anything to do with anyone who hadn't lost a baby," my cousin Jenny said. "Others don't understand."

People also say really dumb things. One guy said, "Well, I guess God changed His mind, huh?"

Exhale.

Uncurl fist.

How many ways can people knowingly or unknowingly sucker punch us? The surprising and sad list of knock-you-out comments below reveal the many ways people hurt us when we're the most fragile. Being forewarned will help you put up your guard and deflect killer blows to your heart, plus serve as a what-not-to-say to the unaware.

When showered by a confetti of hurtful remarks, brush off those below belt blows and the verbal upper cuts that knock you down for the count. When the fact heavers, look-on-the-bright-siders, fixers, blamers, minimizers, pious , or comparison-makers offer their flab-bergaster comments, laugh to your self and think: *Oh right, that's what you're* **not** *supposed to say.*

The following statements reflect common remarks people say to miscarriage moms.

- At least it happened earlier and not later.
- At least it wasn't actually a baby.
- At least now you know you can get pregnant.
- At least you didn't know or bond with the baby.
- Be thankful for the child or children you have.
- At least the fetus didn't have a soul yet.

"God did not make death, and He does not delight in the death of the living. For he created all things so that they might exist. God created us for incorruption, and made us in the image of his own eternity, but through the devil's envy death entered the world."

Wisdom of Solomon: 1:13-15, 2:23-24.

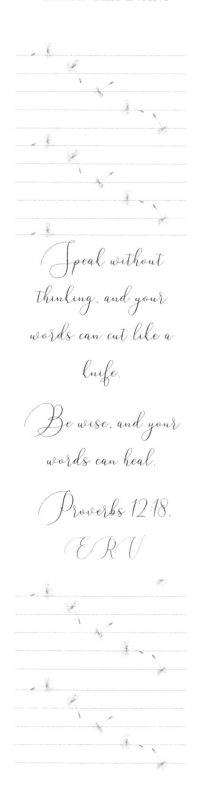

Speak without thinking, and your words can cut like a knife.

Be wise, and your words can heal.

Proverbs 12:18.
ERV

- Caring for a special needs child is expensive.
- Did the doctor say what was wrong with you or the baby?
- Did you do something you weren't supposed to?
- Do you have sin in your life? This wouldn't have happened otherwise.
- You need to lose some weight before trying again.
- Nature has a way of taking care of mistakes.
- You can try again.
- Don't worry, you'll have another baby.
- Everything happens for a reason. It's for the best.
- Get over it and move on.
- God doesn't give us more than we can handle.
- God gives and God takes away.
- God has a plan. It's not up to us to question His reasons.
- God needed another angel in heaven.
- God works all things together for the good of those who love Him.
- Have you considered adoption?
- Have you ever thought about not having any children?
- Have you gotten checked for . . . ?
- Hopefully it was a girl since you wanted a boy.
- I completely understand how you feel.
- I didn't know you were trying to get pregnant.
- I experienced a stillbirth, which is worse than a miscarriage.
- I'm sure you'll feel better soon.
- It happens. It could be worse.

- In my day we just treated it like a heavy period.
- It happened for a reason.
- It just wasn't meant to be.
- It must have been God's will.
- It probably wasn't a miscarriage, just a bad period.
- It wasn't your time.
- It's for the best.
- It's the best thing given the situation.
- Just pray about it.
- Maybe you should or shouldn't have . . .
- Miscarriage is really common. You'll be okay.
- My cousin's miscarriage was worse than yours.
- My friend had two miscarriages and now has two healthy kids.
- No one ever said life would be easy.
- Something was wrong with your baby.
- This too shall pass.
- Time will heal everything.
- Stop feeling sorry for yourself.
- When you have a baby, you won't imagine life with a different child.
- You have too many kids already.
- Relax. Quit worrying. Your body will do it when it's ready.
- Your body's getting too old to carry a child.
- You should not have told anyone you were pregnant until after the first trimester.
- You'll forget one day.
- You wouldn't want a baby with issues.
- You'll feel better in a few days.
- You'll get pregnant again.

"What helped me most was

a hug.

a listening ear.

a sympathetic heart.

a homemade meal.

an "I'm sorry for your loss."

Amy, California.

Member of the Love Letters to Miscarriage moms Facebook Page

- You'll never be ready for a baby.
- You're not ready to be somebody's mom yet.
- Your baby is in a better place.
- Your baby was too good for earth.
- Your body was just doing its job.
- You're young. Enjoy life while you can.

How many of the aforementioned comments caught you unaware and drove a stake into your heart?

Spend your fleeting energy on recovering hope. Release the anger and guilt you may feel toward their good fortune of never experiencing a miscarriage. Give your loved ones the benefit of the doubt: They mean well.

Yet, be intentional about seeking connections with people who understand what you're going through.

The days following my miscarriage gave the No Good Bad Most Terrible Day a run for its money. A week after the miscarriage, I visited Lona in the living room of her farmhouse. Beyond the window, vacant rows of a quarter-acre garden reminded me of winter's fast approach.

Lona's twins would have been 23 years old. As if her miscarriages occurred 23 days ago, Lona's onslaught of tears shocked me.

"Sam," she managed. "You're the first person who ever asked me about what happened. You're the first person who's ever tried to understand what I went through."

My lips parted. *You've never talked about this with anyone in 23 years?* My parents' generation shakes its finger at my generation for our virtual communication.

Yet, many Baby Boomers I spoke with share this commonality: They suffered their miscarriages in silence. When they needed community the most, a social taboo pressured them to remain quiet.

Share your story. I can't stress this enough. You'll release your hurt. You may also facilitate the healing in other women's lives.

As Lona and I shoved the tissue box back and forth between us, I asked, "What did you need to hear back then?"

"Nothing! I didn't want to hear any of the sorry, gushy, mushy yaza-yaza stuff."

She scored a point for making me laugh. "Can I quote you?"

Quoted Lona. Check.

I reflected on my sucker puncher experiences. Staring at me with wide, Labrador eyes, an acquaintance inhaled a quick intake of breath. The attempt at profound wisdom crept up her vocal chords.

A flash of panic welled within me, followed by two thoughts: 1. *Please, don't say whatever you're about to say! 2. Will the words heal me?*

By the time she finished speaking, I tried not to visibly wince at the affect of her well-meaning speech. *I should have chosen number 1.*

Magical words can't replace the loss, or return our babies to us. However, each time a miscarriage mom whispers, "I know what you're going through . . ." her confession coats my wound with a thin layer of salve.

Several times a person declared, "I know what you're going through. I lost my dog—eighty-year-old father—three-legged gerbil named Skippy."

If you've fallen upon an effective comeback for poor, deceased Skippy, please, let me know. Skippy-like comments drove me underground in search of the 'Been There' Secret Society.

I mentioned to my friend Lona, "A week has passed since the miscarriage and I finally stopped bleeding. I wiped myself after going to the bathroom and practically cheered—"

". . . because there was no more blood."

I sighed with relief. Finally! A woman on the same page as myself. If our culture never speaks about miscarriage, then speaking about the amount of blood expelled is unheard of.

Yet, Lona knew.

Lona's eyes pooled and overflowed. "At least if we bled for children who lived, the hemorrhaging would be worthwhile."

"Agreed. The blood taunted me. I could almost hear my body jeering. 'Neenner neenner boo boo, you lost your baby!'"

We laughed and cried together. Comments we cracked would shock a non-Been There.

So how do you kill a conversation with the non-Been There's in your life? Most likely some don't know what to say, but feel compelled to say something, even when it's the last thing you want to hear. Even well-intentioned non-Been There's simply don't know the right words to say to comfort you.

Don't be afraid to say, "I'm sorry, I'm just not up to talking about this right now. It's too painful."

What if . . .

- a person continues to talk and fails to honor your straightforward request? Cut them off: "I'm struggling with a devastating loss and prefer not to talk about it any further."

- an insensitive person makes statements that are rude, inaccurate, or blame you? Walk away. You already have too much to deal with physically and emotionally to waste energy reasoning away unhelpful inaccuracies.

- a difficult person traps you in an uncomfortable conversation? Plaster on a straight face and refuse to engage in conversation that invites more commentery. Allow their comments to pass through you.

- someone you can't avoid offers unsolicited advice or unhelpful comments? Ask a friend or family member to run interference and keep them away from you.

An acquaintance volleyed the conversation toward me in an effort to elicit details I didn't feel like sharing. My brain stalled on a conversation I shared with a non-Been There. In mid-sentence, mid-word, I simply stopped talking.

After an awkward pause, she said, "Uh, okay. Well, I'm just going to go back to my lunch then."

I should have apologized. When she walked away, I just felt too relieved.

Find the Been There's in your life. What does a Been There look and sound like? A Been There:

- respects your privacy
- keeps your confidences

Speak without thinking,
and your words
can cut like a knife.

Be wise, and your
words can heal.

Proverbs 12:18.
ERV

- listens without judgment
- allows you to lead the conversation
- supports your need to talk
- doesn't monopolize the conversation.

Reflection: What's On My Heart?

Have well-intentioned people spewed comments that rankled you or even caused you more pain? Vent below:

Name the 'Been There's' you can call. List their names and phone numbers below. If you don't know anyone to call, call a counselor, or find a support group in your community, online, or in a closed Facebook group. Search for "Rainbow babies" or "Miscarriage Support."

In the Words of Others

Hey, Sister,

The word "miscarriage" filled me with more pain, anger, and sense of loss than any other word in the English language. At 28 years old, I had two miscarriages within a year of each other. The miscarriages wrecked my body's chance of getting pregnant.

People I love meant well. They tried to uplift me. But let me tell you ladies, some people should really filter what they think before it spills outta their mouths.

"Trust in God's plan." Really? Not only did I lose my babies, I also lost the chance to create future babies. I wanted to throw something at the multiple people who said that to me as I screamed, "How could this be God's plan for me? How could you say that to me?" Unhelpful!

"At least you are healthy." Oh dear person who just said that to me, do you even know the heartbreak of losing a child? This encouragement made me want to vomit.

I was healthy, but my unborn children obviously weren't. As a mother, I would have gladly exchanged my life for theirs.

"Look at the silver lining and stay positive." How in the Mighty Name of Jesus Christ does a mother "see a silver lining" or "stay positive" after losing a child! Come on already! Did you honestly think that was a good thing to say in that moment?

People have and will continue to offer brainless advice. Compare notes, and laugh with and receive validation from other women who understand.

There's a whole mess of people out there who don't get it. But there are plenty of women who do. You are not alone. I've Got Your Back, Woman.

Erin

Pennsylvania

9 Post-Miscarriage Firsts

Two weeks following the miscarriage, Clint's heavy, size 13 feet pounded up the steps of the back porch. My fingers hovered above the keyboard, waiting. I cringed in anticipation. Please don't slam . . .

. . . the wooden screen door in the kitchen slapped against the frame.

I could not yet see Clint. However, nothing about my husband was subtle. One shoe thudded to the floor. The next bounced a bit, indicating a flick of the foot.

Tomorrow he'll tell me he can't find one of his shoes.

A plastic shopping bag swished and dropped to the floor. Crusty silverware trapped within a plastic container rattled. The clunk of the Rubbermaid container tumbling into the sink never sounded. *Ugh. Man-child.*

When I heard him behind me, I spun around in my chair. "How was work?"

"Good." He lifted his eyebrows and chin and glanced toward the computer. "You get a lot done today?"

"I did, actually."

"So, when do we get to have sex again?"

"Tonight works."

"Okay." He left the room. I resumed typing.

Time out. Are you thinking, *This woman's husband dumps his stuff all over the floor, doesn't pick up after himself, and that turns her on? I'd be like, dude, get your sweaty gym shoes off the kitchen floor and then we'll talk.*

Well, your thoughts aren't far off. Clint and I pivoted many arguments around the topic of his cleanliness—or lack thereof. That night the mess didn't register, not really.

Here's a glimpse into my brain at that moment:

- *The doctor said, "No sex until the first period."*
- *Will my fears affect my performance or his?*
- *Has the miscarriage altered our intimate connection?*

These thoughts vied for attention, but this thought trumped them all:

God, I am revved and ready.

No one shared the "We're on a Sex Strike" memo with my libido. Prior to the miscarriage, Clint and I made love frequently. So, for us, two weeks seemed like a loooooooonnnng time.

Sex required courage as we made love that night. The pregnancy loss did not affect performance.

Condom . . . That thought floated away before my brain finished thinking the word. During sex is not the most opportune time to bring up protection. I remembered mumbling, "God's will be done," more accurately translated, "the hell with it."

However, my other apprehensions butted against reality. I feared getting pregnant and not getting pregnant. Engaging in sex reminded me that we lost the child we created. That first sexual encounter also revealed to me the transformation of our intimate connection. As I held my husband and felt his bare back beneath my hands, our shared loss struck me.

Our love created a child. *Our, us, we.* We connected to conceive a child. We were connected by the loss. Sex reminded me that I was pregnant. Our connection reminded me that I was not alone.

The next morning, I counted. I whipped out a calendar and pressed my finger into the little boxes.

Oh, no.

"Maybe we shouldn't have had sex last night."

The doctor's instructions rang like an alarm bell: "Protected sex prior to your first period."

I winced.

In the days following, my body acted abnormally. I experienced mild cramping and sore nipples.

Am I imagining these pregnancy symptoms because I want to be pregnant so desperately?

The doctor called me into her office to measure my hCG levels one more time.

For four days, I carried a secret hope. *Maybe I'm pregnant again.*

I imagined the doctor calling to say, "Shame on you, Mrs. Evans, for engaging in unprotected sex with your husband. Also, congratulations. My educated guess for your due date is . . . "

On Day 5 of post-first-sex-after-loss, I awoke to

the phone ringing. I felt better than I had in days, if numb is considered progress.

"Mrs. Evans?"

"Yes?" I yawned.

"This is the doctor's office. Your lab results are back."

Fully awake, fully alert, emotion welled within me like a dam about to burst.

"Your hCG levels are decreasing as they should."

Blood work. Numbers going down . . . down? The news impacted me like a head on collision with a semi-truck. My muscles tightened. My chest stung. My eyes blinked back tears.

Click. End of call.

I stared at the phone. My breath sounded like someone else's. Then an invisible vacuum sucked sound from the room.

I snapped out of my fugue state and slipped my phone into my pocket. Time sojourned on, I plastered a brave expression on my face and resumed my routine.

Lucky us, we experience all the side effects of post-pregnancy—minus our child. The bleeding. The hormones. The weight gain. The pain. It's a cruel trick, if you ask me, which you didn't.

Miserable, gray clouds sheeted the sky in Lebanon's low valley between Oregon's Coast Range and the Cascade Range. The gloomy sky contributed to my mournful mood. More often than not, clouds skated from the peaks of one mountain range to the pinnacles of the other, offering the valley mild glimpses of the sun. Locals refer to the patches of light as "sun breaks." No sun breaks soothed my overcast spirit that day.

Apparently, symptoms of pregnancy and the symptoms of PMS—mild cramping and sore nipples —are much the same.

I snorted. Earlier in my pregnancy, Clint threw his hands in front of him, then jerked his body from side to side, then up and down, shouting, "Wheeeeeee!" I tried not to laugh, wishing his description weren't right on the money.

But now I shuttered with dread at the thought that *this* terrifying roller coaster ride would never end.

Are you terrified of sex? Terrified of getting pregnant? Terrified of not getting pregnant? Terrified of the act itself? Terrified that sex will remind you that you were pregnant and are no longer? All of these are normal emotions.

My first sexual encounter after a miscarriage hurt emotionally. However, you'll know when you're both ready. Eventually the need for sex outweighs the fear.

The First Period: If you listen to your doctor, you'll get a period after the miscarriage. We're not supposed to get our periods. We're supposed to be pregnant. Our period is one more painful reminder we aren't pregnant anymore.

That first period, as well as many thereafter, lands a hard blow. Each cycle represents a non-pregnancy. Each period zombified me.

Misty recalled with vehemence how her cycles made her feel. "I've never felt so much emptiness in my entire life—ever."

The First Weeks: Everything inside you will feel like sludge.

Po-we-ring dooooowwwwn . . .

Though I lost weight with the miscarriage, I swiftly added on even more pounds via fast food and couch-potato-itis. Like me, you might wish you struggled with the type of depression wherein you don't eat.

At this point my dad's brilliant advice from childhood haunted me. When dad caught my sisters and I glued to the TV screen, he jokingly said, "Do something, even if it's wrong."

Now I'm telling you . . . do something, even if it's wrong. Seriously, move. Don't feel guilty on your sluggish days. Really try your best to leave the house, even just to walk down the block and back.

By all means, eat lots of chocolate. Drive to your favorite fast-food restaurant and order "the usual" without guilt. Indulge yourself. However, at a certain point, force yourself to make healthy choices.

When staying inside the house for forty-eight hours straight satisfies you—fight the urge to do nothing. Get up. Fight for your health.

Painful Firsts: Seemingly days after my miscarriage announcement a friend changed her profile picture to the 20-week ultrasound photo of her unborn daughter. My heart clunked. Tears stung.

How dare she! Doesn't she know how much pain I'm in?

I contemplated a hateful message.

I wondered. *Should I ask her to remove the picture?*

I considered blocking her.

I chose, instead, to stay away from Facebook for a while. All these cutesy couples getting pregnant. *Great for them.* The void at my center, mixed with jealousy, churned up a thick nausea.

Spend a limited amount of time on social media. "I'm pregnant" announcements and "Here's my little bundle growing" bump shots on social media will scrape raw your pain.

Our friends shouldn't hide from us, but we don't want to invite opportunities to compound our pain, either. Stay off social media until you're ready to log back in. If the only Facebook posts you relate to are written by other miscarriage moms, visit closed Facebook group pages for miscarriage support and try to avoid scrolling through your Facebook news feed.

The hardest phone call came the January following the miscarriage. My younger sister, who married after me, called to tell me, "I'm pregnant."

The conversation was difficult for both of us. She feared calling me but didn't want me to find out through Facebook.

My reply came out in a low monotone. "Congratulations, Jorie. I'm happy for you." The words were true, but the admission cost me. Even two time zones apart, I couldn't hide the torment. "I know I don't sound like I'm happy for you, I really am, I just . . . "

"No, I know, 'Sman-tha'. I understand. I just wanted you to know."

I ended the call shortly thereafter, to grant each of us reprieve, then proceeded to bawl my eyes out.

I held my new niece, Ella Bella Bear, a couple

My friends, don't be surprised at the painful things that you are now suffering, which are testing your faith.

Don't think that something strange is happening to you.

*1 Peter 4:12.
ERV*

weeks after the one-year anniversary of my miscarriage. I kissed her cheek.

"Did you see your cousin in passing, on the way down from heaven?" I pressed my index finger into her curled fist. "I love you, little girl, but you'll never understand that you shouldn't be the oldest grandchild." I wiped my eyes before Jorie noticed my tears dripping onto her child.

Ten years later, the memory of holding Ella that first time still causes me to cry. Ten years later, the birth order of the grandchildren still stings. Sometimes, the hurt stings less.

In the months following the miscarriage, I must have emitted a frequency that caused pregnant women to keep their distance from me. I don't remember seeing many pregnant women.

I also went out of my way to avoid them. A preschool was connected to the church where I worked. The main doors led into an atrium with the preschool off to the right and the church offices on the left.

Days after the miscarriage, I emerged from the offices into the atrium at the same time a pregnant mother escorted her preschool-aged son into the building. I caught a glimpse of her long dark hair swept back into a ponytail, a flowing white shirt covering her beautifully rounded belly, and a little boy's hand tucked into her own.

Uh uh. I shook my head and executed an about face. *Not happening.* At that moment I resolved not to use the main entrance of the church when preschool was in session. The small change—that non-Been There's might have thought petty— helped immensely. By removing myself, I spared my grieving heart an unnecessary trigger. Protect your heart from exposing yourself to painful pregnancy reminders.

The First Baby Shower: One friend wrote to me about the first baby shower she attended following her miscarriage. I'm passing the wisdom from her experience on to you.

> *Sam, I was happy for my friend, but I was in agony the entire time I spent at her baby shower. When tears threatened to break through the dam of my loss, I swallowed each lump in my throat. And shopping for her gift? I wanted to curl into a fetal position in the baby aisle and just sob.*

Guard your emotional health. This is one time in life to place your self-care before pleasing others.

Call the hostess and explain, "I just miscarried and I'm not up to attending. It's too painful. Give my love to [insert name of pregnant mom]."

If you don't have the energy to make the call, ask a friend to call the hostess.

Shield yourself. The people in your world will understand that you're grieving.

- Decline a baby shower invitation with an apology.
- Send a cash gift with a friend rather than shopping in the baby aisles for the perfect gift.
- Or shop online and mail a gift.

You are loved, Mom. Let who you are at this moment be enough.

First Mother's Day: Mother's Day triggers many feelings: fear, guilt, dread, self-doubt, envy, anxiety. On your way to becoming a mother, your

child's life was cut short. Mother's Day implies that a 'mother' cares for a living, breathing child. Many feel like 'secret' mothers. Many moms express feeling isolated, lonely, left out, cheated, misunderstood, and empty. The day you looked forward to celebrating is now dreaded, because you lost what you thought made you a mother and gifted you with the title of mother.

The second Sunday in May recognizing motherhood remains a tough day for women who:

- mourn a miscarriage, stillbirth, or infant death
- grieve the loss of their mother who died
- lament estrangement from their mom
- suffer from infertility
- are older, unmarried and pine for a child.

A friend, who prefers to remain anonymous, sent me this Mother's Day story.

My sister, who suffers with multiple mental illness diagnoses, had four abortions, one miscarriage, and never birthed a child. She longed for love from her child. In spite of her mental health, her tenderness and loving heart toward children, especially my children, was evident. One year, I sent her a Mother's Day card acknowledging her babies who resided in heaven in the arms of their grandfather, our dad. My sister cried as she thanked me, because no one had ever acknowledged her children or motherhood.

A barrage of in-your-face reminders—greeting cards, commercials, and social media—celebrate the Hallmark 'perfect' picture, 1950s retro mom. If you feel like a mother, how do you celebrate Mother's Day when you have no children others can see? It's complicated. If you're questioning the title of 'mom,' two parallel lines on a pregnancy test were proof positive that you're a mom.

The visible—stretch marks, photo albums, baby teeth, and greasy finger prints on glass—can't extinguish the invisible—the imprint your child left on your mother's heart. Carrying a child in your womb changed you.

You conceived, carried, loved, and protected your baby for his or her entire life. Own the title. Mother's Day belongs to you.

Even if you grew up sitting on a church pew every Sunday, the minister's sermon, or the priest's blessing, or the dedication of babies on Mother's Day, or the tradition of asking moms to stand up is beyond agonizing. If you do attend church on Mother's Day, stuff your purse with tissues and refrain from applying mascara.

If going to church or getting together with family is too difficult, make other plans with those who understand you're in mourning. Give yourself grace and avoid doing anything that makes the day harder than it already is. And don't forget your baby's father who grieves differently than you. He's at a loss to know what to do or what to say or how to support you.

Share your feelings about Mother and Father's Day with your child's father. Acknowledge his fatherhood. Talk with another mom who

There will be a day maybe a year or so from now when you realize you didn't think about the miscarriage.

More time will pass and you'll realize you haven't thought about the miscarriage for three or four days.

Mary

experienced pregnancy or child loss. Say your sweet child's name and acknowledge that you're mothers.

It's okay to not be okay. It's okay to ugly cry and to mourn the child you miss or never grieved. Even if your first hello was goodbye, your pain, your mourning, your love, and your child matters.

On Mother's Day, celebrating the arrival of a healthy baby lessoned my pain of missing the child I lost. However, a new baby didn't erase the pain of a pregnancy loss.

However you choose to ignore or celebrate Mothers' Day, honor your motherhood.

#You'reWorthIt

#NeverForget

#YouAreAMom

My First Outing: A couple weeks after the miscarriage, I forced myself to leave the house for a few hours. I landed on Lori's couch and clung to her heating pad like a lifeline as I tried to explain the actual miscarriage.

"Then this huge glob . . . " I motioned with my hands.

"Liver," she finished. "That's what the tissue reminded me of."

"Yeah," I agreed. We spoke in her living room for nearly two hours.

Talking helped me the most. Lori and I were such good friends that she easily diverted my attention with casual conversation.

That day, her washing machine broke with two sons in the midst of their football season. She described the visceral image of lugging all their sweat-and-mud-soaked clothing to the laundromat. That mundane conversation about dirty laundry felt like breathing in fresh air, not unlike the fresh smell of clean laundry.

Mourning blindsides you. The following are a few suggestions from miscarriage moms I spoke with following my loss:

- Talk about what happened to the people you want to talk with, only when you want to talk.
- If you're already a mom, find a babysitter at least one day a week. Dia said, "I couldn't 'cope' really. I had kids to take care of." Jenny, Lona, and Monica expressed similar sentiments.
- Don't feel guilty if you're a teensy bit emotional.
- Don't feel like you owe the people around you a happy, perky put-together persona. Anyone who expects this of you is an idiot. Even my husband can tell you that.
- Cry often. Crying releases endorphins and toxins. I always feel so much more at peace after a good cry.
- Use caution when watching TV or movies. Google your movie choices to avoid shows depicting miscarriage scenes, which will knock the wind out of you. *The Help* and *The Time Traveler's Wife* caught me off guard. For a list of movies to avoid, check out my website, LoveSamEvans.com/books.

Friend, be gentle and kind with yourself. Grant yourself grace.

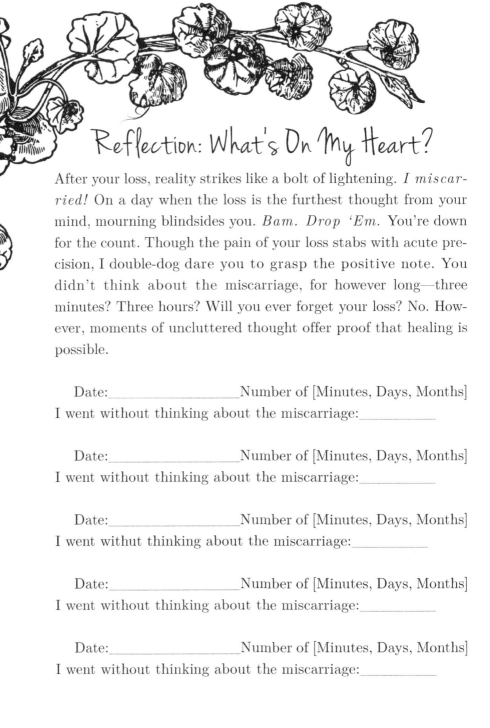

Reflection: What's On My Heart?

After your loss, reality strikes like a bolt of lightening. *I miscarried!* On a day when the loss is the furthest thought from your mind, mourning blindsides you. *Bam. Drop 'Em.* You're down for the count. Though the pain of your loss stabs with acute precision, I double-dog dare you to grasp the positive note. You didn't think about the miscarriage, for however long—three minutes? Three hours? Will you ever forget your loss? No. However, moments of uncluttered thought offer proof that healing is possible.

Date:_____Number of [Minutes, Days, Months] I went without thinking about the miscarriage:_____

Date:_____Number of [Minutes, Days, Months] I went without thinking about the miscarriage:_____

Date:_____Number of [Minutes, Days, Months] I went withut thinking about the miscarriage:_____

Date:_____Number of [Minutes, Days, Months] I went without thinking about the miscarriage:_____

Date:_____Number of [Minutes, Days, Months] I went without thinking about the miscarriage:_____

In the Words of Others

Hey Sister,

Today was our little one's due date. I feel like there's always something to remind me that we lost a baby. When we started trying for a baby, we were so excited. We had so much joy last summer when we found out we were pregnant! It seems like yesterday, but it also seems so far away that joy can't be recaptured.

I still wonder why it felt so right in July if it really wasn't part of God's plan for us. It's hard for me to see God working in my life. Eight months ago, we were excited to buy our own house. Eight months ago, we were excited to become parents. Eight months ago, we thought God was guiding us. Today, I don't feel like God even cares.

Yesterday, the doctor said I would be a good candidate for Clomid, a drug that could help me ovulate (and double the risk of miscarriage). He said while a normal couple usually gets pregnant in less than one year, for me it is much less likely. "Five years," he guessed.

I hate that Satan lies. He's been trying to convince me that trying to be a mother doesn't matter. That losing my child doesn't matter. But it does matter. My heart is broken and he tries to tell me, "It's not a big deal; get over it."

It's healthy to share our struggles, I know, but I just fear what others will say. People just don't understand unless they've been through it too. It's hard for people to understand that it's more than a lost child.

It's knowing you flushed your baby down the toilet. It's months of trying with no results. It's months of knowing what's wrong with you. It's months of frustration and sadness. Months of bitterness and a hardening heart. Months gone by of other people becoming pregnant and having babies. Months of people unknowingly giving me worthless and hurtful advice about when to start a family. Months of waiting, trying to be patient, but just being confused. Months of hoping to receive from God.

Months of NO. NO. NO. I'm so tired. I miss you, Little One.

LeAnna, Oregon

10 The Fire of Mourning

The day after the miscarriage, I grabbed at my chest near where my heart supposedly beat, feeling devoid of life. My lungs constricted making it difficult to breath. The gentle encouragement of my cousin Angela on the other end of the phone fizzled away like the crackle of a static-laced radio connection.

I catapulted from the chair, and spoke to Clint while clasping the phone to my ear. "I'm going to burn things."

"What?" I heard in surround sound as Clint and Angela replied in unison.

I rolled my eyes. *Come on, brain. You can do this. Remember when you used to articulate complete sentences all by yourself?* I struggled to piecemeal words together in my head before speaking out loud. The amount of effort speaking required frightened me.

"I'm going to the backyard to burn yard debris in our fire pit. Working with my hands will help me refocus, and I think staring into the flames will calm me down."

As I walked toward the door, I called over my shoulder, "Hey Clint, next time, can, 'I'm going to burn things' be enough words?"

When you go through deep waters and great trouble. I will be with you.

When you go through rivers of difficulty. you will not drown!

When you walk through the fire of oppression. you will not be burned up the flames will not consume you.

Isaiah 43:2. TLB

"Probably not," Clint replied.

Angela laughed throughout our exchange.

Despite balancing the phone between my ear and shoulder, I built up substantial flames with little trouble using branches from an overgrown Cherry Laurel hedge I'd recently chopped back. As I spoke to Angela, I tossed branch after branch into the flames.

I discovered with delight that the wide, oily leaves proved highly flammable. Each time I threw a branch onto the pile, I leapt away from the flash fire. Just as I expected, the flames calmed me.

I lost Angela's words within the rustle of leaves. I shifted the position of the phone and nearly hit myself in the face with a three-foot-long branch.

"What did you—" I jerked my head back in reflexive movement and the phone slipped from my shoulder and tumbled into the fire. "Oh, no! Angela! I dropped you into the fire!"

Without thinking, I reached down and pinched the phone between the pads of my thumb and forefinger. "Ouch!"

I dropped my cell a second time intentionally, this time swinging it toward the crusted earth outside the fire pit. Metallic rainbows like gasoline on water swirled on the keypad. Cracks webbed across the screen.

A double take later, I realized the call was still active. I tested the temperature and picked up the phone with caution. "Angela?"

"Yeah?"

"I dropped you into the fire."

"I heard."

"You seem okay, though. Are your clothes singed?"

We laughed.

My fire-branded phone looked a lot like me—cracked, broken. The fire altered me, too. Dialing numbers on the keypad required force, but my phone was still useable.

Two years before my miscarriage, our spring retreat theme was "Under Construction." On the back of the T-shirts, the words within a caution diamond warned: "God at work."

Beneath the diamond sat "Zechariah 13:9," our theme verse for the retreat:

> *"This third I will bring into the fire. I will refine them like silver and test them like gold. They will call upon me and I will answer. I will say, 'They are my people' and they will say, 'The LORD is our God.'"*

After I ended the call with Angela, my thoughts drifted to Zechariah 13:9. As I stared into the flames in my backyard fire, I poured myself into the fire like liquid gold. Fashioned by grief, the following poem emerged.

The heat presses against me with physical force. Though I shy away, the flames surround me and I am unable to escape.

I am not burning alive, but rather burning within.

An open wound to an open flame.

A brand cauterizes my heart.

I cry out.

God, please save me!

But people are born to have trouble, as surely as sparks rise from a fire.

Job 5:7. ERV

The thunk, thunk, thunk of a hammer with accurate aim jostles my frame.

I shift in discomfort. I cringe.

The assault damages me.

Am I damaged?

No.

Not damaged, but different. I am changed.

My tears evaporate. I understand. For now, my place is in the fire.

Tongs clasp my frame and draw me deeper, toward the core of the heat.

I am lifted and spun.

Fear melts away.

Vanity and shame flare up in flame.

Whatever focus I spared on inconsequential matters fades into the gray.

Only worthwhile is the fire around me and the flame within.

Through licks of orange I see Him.

I glimpse the Almighty.

Tears shimmer in His eyes like diamonds.

His calloused hand, blackened with soot draws me from the furnace. With two rough hands He gently gathers me at His chest. I feel the solid beating of His heart and glance down at the brand upon my own.

A thumbprint is emblazonedd there.

His.

I am not the same, but I am forever, wholly loved, wholly changed.

I am baptized by fire.

I am His.

Life kept moving; so did my job. Just before teaching youth group one night, I withdrew my phone, covered in second degree burns, from my pocket to text someone. Levi noticed my phone and yanked the device away from me to investigate.

"Why don't you just buy a new one?" Nick demanded, gaping over his shoulder.

"Because this one still works." I stretched my arm toward my phone. Levi skittered just beyond my reach.

Reality snapped and fizzled. Like a moth to flame powerful memories dragged me back to the day following the miscarriage. Grief swirled like nausea.

Nick grabbed the phone. "Her contacts still work!"

"Seriously?" Levi jabbed him in the ribs with his elbow.

A headlock came next, followed by an—I-Don't-Know-What. Phone forgotten, they dropped to the ground, laughing and maneuvering.

Any excuse to wrestle. My miscarriage laid aside, I actually laughed.

As the responsible adult in the room, I broke up the match—by kicking their legs. "All right, all—"

"Hey! Ow!" They grinned and helped one another to their feet.

Without trying, without even comprehending my pain, their antics whipped me from the brink of grief as if yanking *me* from the fire.

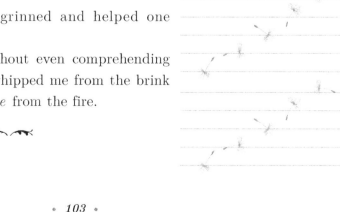

Death took my child, and God received my child.

I am

Through the eyes of miscarriage, I re-read the story of an enraged king who ordered a furnace be fired up seven times hotter than usual. King Nebuchadnezzar's strong soldiers bound Shadrach, Meshach, and Abednego. Nebuchadnezzar was in such a rush, the intense heat from the flames killed the men who threw Shadrach, Meshach, and Abednego into the fiery furnace.

I *love* what happened next in this story. The fire didn't kill Shadrach, Meshach, and Abednego, as expected. As if the oppressive heat was no big deal, they strolled around in the furnace.

As the fire and smoke raged and swirled around Shadrach, Meshach, and Abednego, the King exclaimed, "I see *four* men, walking around freely in the fire, completely unharmed!" Then he ordered, "Shadrach, Meshach, and Abednego, servants of the High God, come out here!"

Upon examination of their bodies, the fire had not singed one hair on their heads. Not one scorch mark singed their clothes. They didn't even smell smoky. While God didn't prevent them from being thrown into the fire, He stood beside them. While God didn't prevent my miscarriage, He stood beside me and walked through the emotional fire with me.

God didn't want me to lose my baby. Death took my child, and God received my child. I will repeat this truth as often as necessary. In the fog of grief, that critical truth is difficult to grasp and hold close.

When just surviving each day is a stand-alone accomplishment, the beauty of who we can become on the other side of this fiery trial is nearly impossible to envision. Yet, the crucible of miscarriage can transform us, refine us.

When the haze and smoke of mourning concealed my future and my heart was on fire with pain, I truly believed that God would use the miscarriage to refine me, as the verse says—to draw me closer to Him.

Even though the refining process was unpleasant, He refined me like silver. He tested me like gold. God used my pain to write this book for good— for your good—and, greater still, for His glory.

Reflection: What's On My Heart?

Your body will recover faster than your emotions. The feelings listed below affect how you feel about your loss, immediately and over time.

Normal Feelings After a Miscarriage
Are you...

- **numb?** Disbelief. You don't feel anything at all.
- **shocked and confused?** Especially if there were no signs before the miscarriage that anything was wrong.
- **sad and tearful?** Perhaps suddenly bursting into tears without any obvious trigger.
- **guilty?** Wondering if you caused the miscarriage? That's very unlikely.
- **angry?** At fate? At hospital staff? At others' pregnancy announcements?
- **jealous?** Especially when seeing other pregnant women and babies.
- **empty?** A physical sense of loss.
- **lonely?** Especially when others don't understand.
- **panicky and out of control?** Overwhelmed, unable to cope with everyday life.
- **depressed:** Difficulty concentrating and sleeping, or sleeping too much.

Which feelings best describe where you are today?

Which feelings best describe where you were yesterday, a week ago, a month ago?

October 7: Today I unlocked the door to my office and secretly wished when I opened the door I would stroll into a beautiful, magical place where I could forget everything and feel no pain.

Much to my dismay, when I walked into my office the room was simply that—my office. An overactive imagination can be a dangerous thing. Our God-given imagination might also one day set the world on fire.

Write a poem or your thoughts about your heart in the flames. Email what you write to Sam@LoveSamEvans.com. I may share your poem in my LoveSam Evans' newsletter!

In the Words of Others

Dear Mom and Dad of Heaven-Borns,

My wife and I have had two miscarriages. It burns, doesn't it? The grief of losing a child. The white-hot pain constricted my lungs as if I'd sprinted a marathon and couldn't catch my breath.

I suspect the losses will always burn, but the ache fades with time. I promise. I've survived what you're living through.

So today, I pray for you. I believe God will soothe your ache as he did ours. I pray that your faith will be refined on the other side of this trial. I pray God will send you moments and people that will spare you from the scorching grief.

I've walked in your shoes.

Levi

11 Why God?

For three weeks following my loss, I boycotted Scripture. Prior to the miscarriage, just seeing my Bible provided comfort, like catching the glimpse of an old friend in an unexpected place.

After the miscarriage, I scowled at my duct-taped wonder, as if the physical book itself should have tried harder to prevent my miscarriage.

One day, holding my emotion at bay required all the stamina I could muster. My friend Misty held my shaking body. Tapped out, I blubbered, "How c-could God l-l-let this ha-ha-ppen?"

The classic question, *"How could God let bad things happen to good people?"* consumed me.

"Sam, He's jealous for you. He's fighting for you," Misty's soft voice soothed.

I shook my head, finding myself in foreign territory wherein my reality felt more real than my faith. What I believed about God's goodness didn't align with the tragedy that faced me.

Are you thinking? *That hypocrite! Sam told me to trust God, yet she doubts His plan herself?*

Faith without wrestling with doubt is not faith. As Saint Augustine wrote, "Doubt is but another element of faith."

No matter what ashes and debris I faced in the aftermath, I knew my God stood in the fire beside

me in the furnace raging with grief. And just as God delivered Shadrach, Meshach, and Abednego not only *from* the fire, but *through* the fire, He'd deliver me *from* and *through* mourning's fire.

Misty released me from a hug, keeping her hands wrapped firmly around my arms. "Sam, He's fighting for you," she repeated.

Faith assured me that Misty spoke the truth.

He's jealous for you. He's fighting for you. Are you ready to be blessed?

I wasn't there yet. My anger toward God swelled as if He targeted me for this tragedy.

Are you angry with God, too?

Three weeks after my miscarriage, my boycott on Scripture ended, though not at my say-so.

Try arguing with the all-time argument winner and the omniscient (all-knowing) God of the universe. On your best day, your wisdom is still His foolishness and on your worst day during a "God, why me" episode—you possess the brain capacity of a slug.

Depression dumbed my brain.

"God, why?"

"The Lord gave and the Lord has taken away," Job 1:21b, NASB.

"Why me?"

"God does not show favoritism," Romans 2:11, NIV.

He doesn't point to one woman, "Ooh, I like her more. She'll never experience anything painful. Hmm, that girl there, she's naughty. She deserves a miscarriage."

God does not show favoritism and He's certainly not spiteful.

That left me with my original question. The question you're likely asking as well.

"God, why?"

"Brace yourself like a man, I will question you, and you shall answer me. 'Where were you when I laid the earth's foundation? Tell me, if you understand. Who marked off its dimensions? Surely you know,'" Job 38:3–5, NIV.

As I read through Job 38, I heard Him saying to me, "The universe I created is so much bigger than your tiny orbit. I know you're in pain. I know you don't understand. This world is bigger than you. Isn't it enough to know that the God who created the universe stands by your side, loves you, and wants you to be okay? I'm not going anywhere. Isn't that enough?" For just a moment, it was.

Talk out your hurt with God. He's more fathomless than depression. No matter how you feel or what you think, He can handle the verbal lashing.

If you're relieved, if you're depressed, if you're enraged, just be real with Him. He's super strong and super smart. He's had a lot of practice with this whole God thing.

Besides, He already knows your heart better than anyone—even you. He created you with care and He cares about what's going on. He can help.

My friends, theory proves easier than execution. Whatever assurances I received from God faded like a night-time cough syrup and I returned to my doubts.

In a strange twist, I found my doubt coupled

with arrogance. I grew up in the church and for years, I heard how much God loved me and created me to be special. Yet, somewhere along the way, in error, I believed God loved me *more* than others.

In my mind, "Special" with a capital S transformed into a comparison word. Though I never articulated such, "Special" subconsciously meant elevated above the rest, right?

My stellar church attendance record and outstanding moral fiber convinced me that I was more special to God than others around me. That, sisters, is the definition and heart of a Pharisee— men who thought their white robes and status earned them extra points with God.

Conversely, God's grace is an undeserved and unearned gift. God's grace cannot be earned by human effort, not mine, not yours, not even the prophet and saint, John the Baptist's.

John the Baptist fell into a bit of a pharisaical moment with Jesus, too. The two cousins shared a history dating back to before they were born: John leapt within his mother Elizabeth's womb at the arrival of Mary, who was pregnant with Jesus. (Luke 1:39–45)

Witnessing this level of intimacy between Mary and Elizabeth, I wondered. *How often did Mary and Elizabeth reunite after their sons were born? How often did John and Jesus play together throughout the unrecorded years of Jesus' life?*

In addition, all four gospels, Matthew, Mark, Luke, and John, recount variations of John baptizing Jesus. Jesus and John the Baptist knew one another well.

Concluding that Jesus and John loved one another is not too far a leap. Matthew 11:1–18 reveals a glimpse of the grown-up relationship between Jesus and John.

King Herod unjustly imprisoned John for calling Herod out on his infidelity. (Matthew 14:3–5) In Matthew 11, John sent messengers from prison to Jesus, with this question, "Are you *really* the Messiah?"

Oh, John. I know how you feel.

John grew up with Jesus. He preached about Him, pointed others to Him, and baptized Him in the Jordan River. Did John doubt his second cousin, Jesus, was the Messiah? John's real question was not, "Are you Him, or should we look for someone else?"

John's true question was, "Jesus, am I special to you?"

What's the point of an intimate relationship with the God of the Universe, if not for the fringe benefits, such as a Get Out of Jail Free card?

Did Jesus love John?

Yes.

Could Jesus have saved John from beheading?

Yes.

Then, why didn't Jesus intervene?

I have no idea.

However, here's what I do know: Whether or not Jesus saved or didn't save John was not based on how much Jesus loved John.

Does Jesus love us?

Absolutely.

Could He have saved our babies?

Without a doubt.

So, why didn't He then?

I have no idea.

I trust that Jesus sees the bigger picture. Whether mothers' babies live or die is not based on degrees of God's love for us. We are special to Jesus, and our children are too.

For entertainment, Herod beheaded John at a party. (Matthew 14:6–12, NIV) Following the news of John's death, we read:

> "When Jesus heard what happened, he withdrew by boat privately to a solitary place."

Jesus loved John and mourned for him. Jesus loves us, too, and mourns for and with us.

In Revelation 3:20, MSG Jesus says:

> "Look at me. I stand at the door. I knock. If you hear me call and open the door, I'll come right in and sit down to supper with you."

I don't know where you stand with God. I heard Jesus knocking, but each time I reached to turn the doorknob, I retracted my hand, hesitant of the implications of trusting Him with my future.

I craved absolutes and assurances and doubted that relief of my own design waited on the other side. Still, I heard Jesus calling.

Insert your name or nickname in the following blanks.

"This is _____. I know you're in there, _____." Jesus' voice carries a playful tone as He says, "You can't hold out on me forever. Of the two of us, who do you think has more patience?"

Knock.

Knock.

Knock.

A gentle bump against the door tells you that Jesus just rested his forehead against the wood.

"_____, you're beautiful. And you have a beautiful heart. I'm so sorry you're hurting. I'm so sorry I couldn't give you the answer that you cried out for. If you open up,I can give you the peace that eludes you. I'll be here waiting. I will wait as long as it takes."

Does Jesus' offering feel like a poor excuse for the runner-up prize?

"I don't want peace! I want my baby! I wouldn't need peace, if you'd just given me my baby. If you'd let my baby live."

Silence stretches . . .

When He finally speaks, again, I hear the apology in His tenor. "As long as it takes, _____. As long as it takes, I'm here for you."

In the aftermath of my ground-zero devastation, I felt God's persistent presence almost tangibly. I imagined Him saying, "I'm here, Sam. I'm not going anywhere. You can't get rid of Me. I'm too big. I'm here. You're not alone. You're stuck with Me. And by the way, I love you."

I chose to inch the door open and embrace who awaited me on the other side. I invited Jesus to my table cluttered with my jumbled feelings. I sloughed to the floor my current issues of *Worry* magazine.

For the moment, I shoved aside my thick volumes of *Great Future Expectations*. After all, Jesus has earned the right to a bit of elbow room at my table.

I don't understand why I still hurt.

I don't understand why my wound is not cured and cannot be healed.

Jeremiah 15:18a.

ERV

I eyed the double-edged sword sheathed at His hip. He winked at me and lowered Himself into a chair, unencumbered by the emotional mess piled atop the table.

Love exuded from the shimmering tears He held at bay. Seated across from Him, for a moment, we sat silent together.

I understood that He waited for me to set the pace of the conversation. Without explanation, my heart recognized that what He desired most was honesty.

When I yelled, when I swore, my anger didn't bump Him. He absorbed the pain, dissolved the anger and absolved any offense.

He simply desired authenticity.

Dear friend, no matter what you believe about God or Jesus, I pray that you'll feel the absence of anxiety and rest in the peace layered beneath.

As you read "The Soldiers Three," I pray that you sense God's presence.

The Soldiers Three

There is a Man who walks beside me, our steps are trod in time
When I stumble in the dark His hand reaches out for mine.
Though nights seem cold and lonely, I'll never lose my way
And when I'm afraid, I hold on to that day.

That night so many years ago when I wandered from where I should
But then He came to rescue me and lead me through the wood.
I'll never forget the first sight of His smile or His eyes that beheld such grace
Though the world had waged war with Him, He didn't wear it on his face.

There is a Man who walks before me so I can follow in His steps
He's walked this way, He knows my name, His light shines on the path
Though we face great dangers His sword is always drawn
And though I'm not immune to hurt, the battle wages on.

The trail we tarry is steep and rough but we must sojourn on
There are people lost in darkness hoping that we'll come.
They wear the burdens of their days and pile it on their backs
Their smiles have flattened with the weight of a world that cuts no slack.

There is a Man who walks behind me, my rear guard and battle cry.
He is my source of courage and the Soldier in my eye
The fearless Man tilts His hilt to the enemies who hide
In the shadows of where we have been and the thorny roads that wind.

I will not surrender to the fearful thought of the demons that prowl around
Because I trust the fearless One whose sure steps shake the ground
But I must never think that it's I who scares the cougar
I'm simply a tiny cub with a mother on haunches behind her.

When life is hard and hope is gone and it seems that Satan's won
When darkness is thick and light is scarce and you're too weary to go on
Do not doubt the Soldiers three who won't cease what they've begun
These three love you relentlessly, the Father, Spirit and Son.

Reflection: What's On My Heart?

Choose Your Own Adventure.
In the space below, journal a conversation between you and Jesus.

Congratulations on opening the door to Jesus' knock. Jesus is your warrior-friend, your greatest ally. He loves you fiercely.

I am so proud of you for being honest. Unleashing God in my life terrified me. However, the thought of facing this pain without Him was unbearable.

You may not believe in God, or desire a relationship with Him. But, even if the words you wrote were, "This so is stupid. You're stupid, I don't believe in you," those words, directed toward God, required faith.

If God feels distant, consider the possibility that you closed the door between you. Consider opening the door, or at least cracking open the door a few inches.

In our crazy, chaotic world, it's so easy to believe we're in control. Keeping God in a box feels safer than granting Him free rein in our lives. With God in a box, we never have to grow and change. We never need to step out in freaky faith and believe in the absurd notion of the resurrection of the dead. He wants to resurrect and restore your heart stronger than before.

May you feel His strong arms holding you together. In the stillness, when you're endowed with a peace that passes all understanding, may you find the courage to live with an open heart.

In the Words of Others

Dear Mom,

My heart goes out to you. I know your pain all too well. Our house was very small and run down. The night I miscarried, we had no running water. I used an ice cream pail instead of a toilet. I could not even take a shower, or relax in a bath afterward.

I shouted, "Why God! Why, why, why, and under these conditions!" I sank into a deep depression. I constantly questioned God. How could You let this happen? What did I do to deserve this? My kids suffered. My husband and I became distant. My life was falling apart.

We tried for three years to get pregnant again—and nothing happened. I realized I could no longer let the darkness consume me. I needed peace, and I needed to forgive God. When I invited God back in, God changed my perspective.

I saw that when the miscarriage happened, my husband and I were not in a place to raise another child. Financially, we barely made ends meet. Our living situation was less than ideal. I surrendered to God's plan for my life. I was finally content with being a family of four. I just wasn't meant to have another child, and finally I was okay with that.

Looking back, God also showed me wonderful blessings at work within my life. My husband secured a great job. We were also able to build a beautiful new home, with room for everyone.

I pray that one day you receive your unexpected blessing. After the rain, God promises a rainbow. During the storm, we have to hold tight and keep our strength. We have to believe and trust in God. He knows what He's doing. He has a plan for you too.

Hugs,
Amanda
Lakeville, MN

P.S. I'm due in December!

12 Who's Your Lifeline?

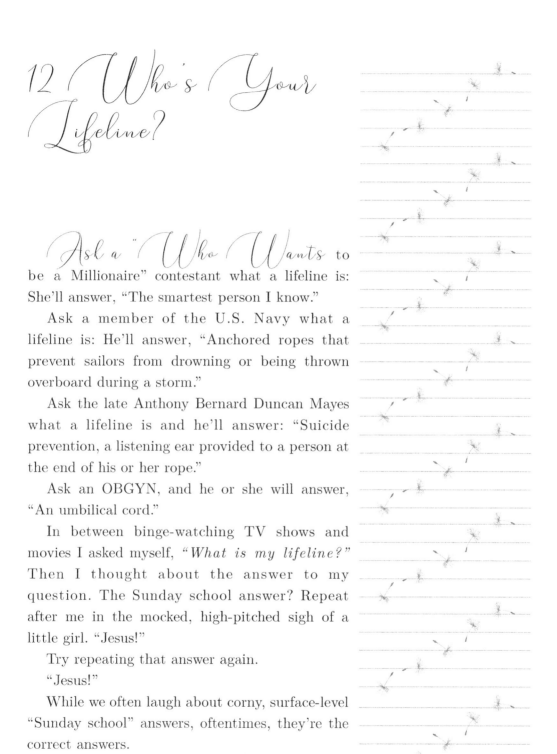

Ask a "Who Wants to be a Millionaire" contestant what a lifeline is: She'll answer, "The smartest person I know."

Ask a member of the U.S. Navy what a lifeline is: He'll answer, "Anchored ropes that prevent sailors from drowning or being thrown overboard during a storm."

Ask the late Anthony Bernard Duncan Mayes what a lifeline is and he'll answer: "Suicide prevention, a listening ear provided to a person at the end of his or her rope."

Ask an OBGYN, and he or she will answer, "An umbilical cord."

In between binge-watching TV shows and movies I asked myself, *What is my lifeline?* Then I thought about the answer to my question. The Sunday school answer? Repeat after me in the mocked, high-pitched sigh of a little girl. "Jesus!"

Try repeating that answer again.

"Jesus!"

While we often laugh about corny, surface-level "Sunday school" answers, oftentimes, they're the correct answers.

Who or what is your lifeline?

Jesus!

The Word of God.

And God Himself.

From Genesis, which means "in the beginning," to Revelation, God bookends the Bible and everything in between.

> *"In the beginning God created the heavens and the earth,"* Genesis 1:1, NASB.

> *"In the beginning was the Word, and the Word was with God, and the Word was God,"* John 1:1, NASB.

> *"I am the Alpha and the Omega,"* says the Lord God, *"who is and who was and who is to come, the Almighty,"* Revelation 1:8, NASB.

> *"'I am the Alpha and the Omega, the first and the last, the beginning and the end,'"* Revelation 21:6; 22:13, NASB.

He existed before the beginning of our world. God created in the beginning. And He will exist the day our world ends.

The second chapter of Genesis describes God giving man life by breathing His own breath into Adam's nostrils. Psalms 139:13, MSG says:

> *Oh yes, you (God) shaped me first inside, then out you formed me in my mother's womb. I thank you, High God—you're breathtaking! Body and soul, I am marvelously made!*

The Creator of galaxies.

The Creator of the angler fish.

The Creator of the blaze of autumn color . . . this same God created you and me.

When our moms birthed us in the delivery room—He rooted for us.

When we learned to speak, to walk, to run—He cheered for us.

When we were gangly, geeky, self-conscious junior high girls—His grin affirmed us.

He saw the treasure in us we had yet to see in ourselves. He loved us through our first boyfriends, our first break-ups, our first broken hearts.

When hurtful choices became our deepest regrets—He grieved for and with us.

When we felt our unspoken and most anxious longings—He understood us.

He knows the best and the worst things about us and still loves us to pieces. As Max Lucado wrote:

> *"If God had a refrigerator, your picture would be on it. If He had a wallet, your photo would be in it. He sends you flowers every spring and a sunrise every morning . . . Face it, friend. He is crazy about you!"*

God, our Creator, just wants to be near us. Emmanuel, meaning 'God with us,' resides with you the middle of your pain, and right now as you read this sentence. Rest in His presence for a moment.

During college, I needed to rest in His presence. Like any good college student, my clean clothes laid on the floor in a separate pile from my

If your heart is broken, you'll find God right there; if you're licked in the gut, he'll help you catch your breath.

Psalm 34:18. MSG

dirty clothes. One evening after a draining guy situation, I lacked the energy and desire to crawl into my lofted bed. I curled into a fetal position on top of my clean clothes and cried myself to sleep.

As I slipped into dreaming, I pictured myself in the palm of God's hand. Feeling safe, protected and loved, I slept like a baby. Shortly thereafter, I sketched in my journal a drawing of myself in God's hand. I will not subject you to that sketch. I can draw a pretty mean stick camel or perhaps a stick sheep. After I miscarried, I drew on my right palm, with black pen, the size and the shape of the child I'd miscarried and held.

I told Jorie, "Look at six-week fetus pictures online." Then I texted her the picture that I drew on my right hand.

Based on my doodle, Jorie, a phenomenal artist, drew the following picture, which became the cover art for the first edition of this book.

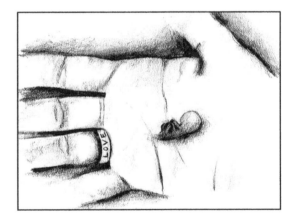

After Jorie drew the picture of the baby in my hand, I came across the drawing in my journal once more. The parallels of Jorie's sketch and mine of me in the palm of God's hand took my breath away. God held me, as my womb held my child.

God still holds me. God also now holds my child in the palm of His hand.

"God with you" is with you right now. He loves you passionately, relentlessly. No matter how far you run or where you hide, you're never beyond God's loving care for you.

He's the hero your heart cries for. He's the soldier standing beside you to protect you. He's the friend, the constant, who's loved you all along. When your world crumbles, He's the solid Rock upon which you can stand.

Some of you may be enraged with God right now. I was when my baby passed from my body into His presence.

I wasn't trying to blame Him. I kept telling myself that God never wanted death. Death took my child away from me.

God received my child on the other side. I repeated this truth in my head, even though my mother's heart wanted none of it. My heart screamed: *If you didn't cause the miscarriage, then why didn't you prevent the loss? Why would you, how could you, give women such a beautiful gift, and then strip them of such blessing?*

My raw outrage demanded a few rounds. I wanted to box God, then throw down the gloves, and hurl haymakers at Him.

But I couldn't deny that even through the gauzy veil of anger, I noticed God at work. The first edition of this book, one of my understandings with God, was evidence of His handiwork.

Despite my love of writing, I didn't trust

Lord, I am so weak. I cried to you all night. My pillow is soaked; my bed is dripping wet from my tears.

Because the Lord has heard my cries, the Lord has heard my request for mercy. The Lord has accepted my prayer.

Psalm 66: 8-9, ERV

---

that I could articulate any intelligible thoughts without divine strength and inspiration. And I hoped that years later those words could touch thousands of lives.

Each time I sat in my chair to write, I begged, "God, I don't want to think about this. I don't want to write about this. So You speak, and I'll just type."

Every day, tears accompanied the typing.

Inhale.

Exhale.

I wrote this book in the midst of my pain so you will not be alone in yours. To be honest, at that time, I didn't feel like writing a book, especially a book about miscarriage—especially a book about my miscarriage. My lifeline, faith, and quirky understanding with God kept my tush in my writing chair.

Under fire, my friend Monica, who's the mother of seven children, spoke words that resonated with obedience. "Sam, I'm just a vessel. God used my body to bring His kids into the world. They're His children."

Monica's insight brought me to a standstill: *I never thought of children as wholly God's before.*

In every other aspect of my life, I strove to allow God's will to prevail. I never pictured giving God my pregnancies and my miscarriages. With seven children, Monica had more practice.

For many of us, this isn't our first encounter with suffering. Following Christ doesn't mean instant success, or instant wealth, or instant get-what-you-want-when-you-want-it.

Following Christ means that when we stumble, or our world falls apart, or we're shattered, our Savior—our life-giver, our life-sustainer, our lifeline—draws us to our feet in the midst of the aftermath of tragedy.

Right now, billions of people in this world hurt for a billion different reasons. God sits above all our pain and devastation, crying for us and along with us. He hurts, because we—His children—hurt. Blinded by pain and in the midst our stubbornness, God's heart aches. We push him away, refusing to allow Him to heal our hearts when He's the only One who can.

God yearns to sustain you, to breathe life into you and to give you His peace that passes all understanding. He offers you rest in the palm of His all-powerful hand.

He wants to be your umbilical cord—your lifeline—to growth, life, health, and healing. An umbilical cord connects a mother and child, delivering oxygen and nutrients to the baby and removing the waste products. Nutrients, the building blocks of growth and repair, provide energy.

Our bodies recover so much quicker than the stream of emotions overwhelming us. As our bodies readjust to not being pregnant, hormonal shifts intensify those emotions. God created our bodies to recover.

Like an umbilical cord, God's love offers a lifeline, providing us with the spiritual nutrients essential for our life, health, and emotional recovery.

Reflection: What's On My Heart?

What or Who is your lifeline? My joking response to that question? "My heating pad," which remained faithfully at my side.

My truest answer? Writing. As my fingers skimmed across the keyboard, my outpoured thoughts granted me relief. My words written to throw a lifeline to someone during her darkest hours lent me purpose.

Think about your lifeline. When you observe or ask other mourners how they survive each day, what coping mechanisms do you notice?

The following feelings are normal responses to a miscarriage. What waste products of miscarriage siphon the emotional oxygen from your life?

Anger	Fear	Out of control
Anxiety	Guilt	Sadness
Confusion	Inadequacy	Self-blame
Depression	Jealousy	Shock
Disappointment	Loneliness	Surprise
Disbelief	Negativity	
Emptiness	Numbness	

Is steam building in your emotional pressure cooker? Ignoring, dismissing, or explaining away your emotions only increases the internal pressure. Read the following healing suggestions, then answer, "How can I take a small step toward healing?"

HEED: Respect your feelings. What is your emotional temperature? Hot? Cold? High? Low? From 1 feeling numb to 10 intense and ready to explode, name and rate your emotions.

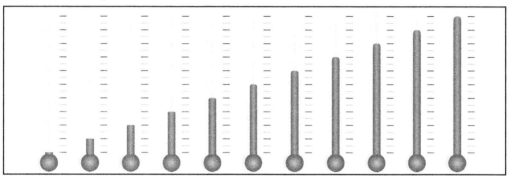

EXHALE: Find a quiet place and still your mind and body. Take one, six-second deep chest breath. Exhale. Ignore all distractions. Draw in another deep breath. Exhale, then ask: What is my body, mind, and spirit telling me?

ACKNOWLEDGE: Listen to yourself. Describe what your heart, mind, and spirit are expressing to you? Take a few minutes to write and articulate "I'm grateful for . . . " If no words flow, choose one uplifting word to focus on today.

LIGHTEN: What can I do today to lighten my burden? Listen to music? Call a friend? Engage in an activity that relaxes me? Take a brisk walk?

What's one small step I *will take* today toward healing?

In the Words of Others

Dear Friend,

I know that you feel lost, angry, and betrayed. You're no longer pregnant. You're not able to hold and love a physical baby. Your arms are empty.

Maybe you're angry because you want your baby so desperately it rocks you to your core while others seemingly carry an unwanted baby to term. Maybe you feel betrayed by your body. This body was supposed to bring a new life and failed you. I've shared all of these same feelings and thoughts.

You are not alone.

The one piece of advice that I offer is to have hope. After years of suffering with infertility, I clung to the hope that if God granted me a pregnancy, although it ended in miscarriage, He would not let me down again.

I hoped God would fill my womb with a new life and that my arms wouldn't always be empty. I hoped that things would work out according to His will, whatever that would be. I hoped that although things looked bleak in the moment, this was only temporary.

Above all, I hoped in God's love for me as His own dear child. Even if I never carry another child, or carry a baby to full term, God created me—me in my mother's womb, for a beautiful purpose.

You are Loved,

Darci

A MOPS Mom

13 Grief, Belief, and Pain Relief

I asked Monica, "May I talk to you about miscarriage?"

"I'd love to! But, Sam, I'm never alone."

Later that week, I climbed into the front seat of her nine-passenger SUV and accompanied Monica as she drove her two oldest children to drama practice.

She glanced into her side mirror and eased into traffic. "I'm not sure I'm the best person to talk to about miscarriage. I wasn't sad."

My breath hitched. *Don't judge. Don't judge. Wait . . . wait for her explanation.*

"When I miscarried, I was raising six children under the age of nine, and I still hadn't recovered from the postpartum depression of my previous pregnancy. Plus, a strange suspicion that I'd miscarry haunted me, so I guarded my heart. The miscarriage didn't surprise me. Also, I was too busy and too hormonal to be sad. Does that make sense? Can we still be friends? Don't judge me, k?"

Makes perfect sense . . . "Yes, of course and I don't."

She laughed. "Good."

We dropped off the kids and headed to a sub sandwich restaurant where she elaborated on her startling-to-me, opening statement, "I couldn't exercise through my pregnancy with Cadence, because of my broken tailbone. Plus my emotions and the delivery were far worse than previous pregnancies."

Monica's back story: Monica broke her tailbone when she was seven months pregnant with her fifth baby, Sidney. Then when Sidney was seven months old, Monica got pregnant again with Cadence and also re-broke her tailbone. *Ouch!*

When Cadence was three months old Monica got pregnant again with the child she miscarried at six weeks and discharged at thirteen weeks. Six weeks later, Monica was pregnant again with Eva, child number seven.

Monica lived in a hormonal whirlwind. She birthed and parented four, then five, then six children while pregnant. The acute pain from her broken tailbone prevented her from lifting and carrying her small children. Monica's overloaded hormones never quite settled before becoming pregnant each time. Sidney was three years old before Monica's depression cloud finally lifted.

"Because of my physical state, I really couldn't grieve," she admitted. "The miscarriage came as a relief." Monica glanced out the restaurant's window deep in thought. "Three years ago, while standing over my kitchen sink, I distinctly remember God saying, 'You'll be tired for three years.' He should've said 'exhausted and emotional.'"

I asked, "I'm so angry about my miscarriage. How were you so accepting of all of that?"

"Throughout the whole disaster, I reminded

myself that God will not give us more than we can handle—with His help."

I dropped my head into my hands. I didn't feel that same assurance. "I'm reaching my breaking point." My chest swelled with a deluge of tears that I choked back. *Not in public. Please not in public.*

Monica continued, "Do you think I remember every time I've washed my family's dishes? That moment lodged itself into my memory, because I was at my breaking point, too. That's why God gave me a time frame. I think God asked you if you're ready to be blessed for the same reason."

"So you think, if God knows we're entering the Red-Zone of our breaking point, He gives us a little heads-up?"

"Exactly. Sam, don't feel guilty about your anger. God can handle your emotions. He created them. He loved me despite my relief about losing a baby. He still loves you. Just focus on getting better."

I forked my hands through my hair and leaned back into my chair, processing.

I understood that each person's story is different, but as we mowed down our sandwiches, Monica's story revealed to me that our responses to our miscarriages are equally unique. The grace of her response taught me that no feelings are irrelevant, or bad, or wrong. Her permission to feel angry, to feel everything without guilt, proved a powerful gift.

Are you angry, too? Are you feeling guilty, or are you relieved?

Maybe you're in high school or college and harboring future dreams.

And when our hearts make us feel guilty,

we can still have peace before God,

because God is greater than our hearts.
He knows everything.

1 John 3:19-20,
ERV

Maybe you're not married to the baby's father, or you hooked up with the wrong guy.

Maybe you're "too old." Raising a child from infancy at your age terrifies you.

Maybe you struggle with addiction, and you're afraid of what drugs could do to your baby.

Maybe you were raped.

Maybe you had medical conditions that complicated the pregnancy.

Maybe you didn't want to lose your supermodel figure.

I don't know your story. I just know your heart struggles enough without suffering at the hands of false guilt. Release that guilt. Even if you drank enough to drown a fish, and you're worried that your habits caused the baby's death, hear this: The miscarriage is not your fault. Plenty of moms intake dangerous amounts of alcohol and drugs while pregnant without any consequence to Mom or baby. The miscarriage was not your fault. If you're relieved, allow yourself to feel relieved.

Your body kicked into survival mode. Your emotions and thoughts—whatever they may be—are your brain's way to work through the healing process.

Survive. Right now, that's your only goal. Lay aside false guilt and shame.

Live day to day. Focus on life to gain a healthy perspective of death and put death in its place. As you struggle to find meaning in your loss, Ecclesiastes 3:1, NIV reminds us:

> *"There is a time for every activity under heaven."*

Grieving has no rules. If you're happy you're not pregnant, don't you dare feel guilty.

Reflection: What's On My Heart?

How is my guilt causing me to punish myself or self-isolate?

How is my guilt preventing me from taking care of myself?

Who will I call to process my false guilt?

In the Words of Others

Dear Momma,

The heaviness you feel on your chest is a weight understood by few. But, you are not alone.

Have you shared your story and received judgment?

Have you remained silent in fear of what others might think or say?

My friend Anne miscarried. A different friend told Anne that her being on birth control killed her baby.

Anne's story and the stories of others' terrified me. So, I kept my secret until I felt like I could burst. I was scared, intimidated by the potential criticism that awaited me.

Finally, I decided my story was worth more than the negative responses of people who might look down on me. The relief I felt was unexplainable and the support I garnered was unexpected.

There are people who will never understand. There are also people whose love is not based on decisions we've made, but the people we are.

You are so loved, Momma. You are cherished. I pray you see yourself as I see you.

Your child is loved eternally by our Father, just as you are. One day we will be reunited with the loves we lost and crave.

For now, hold onto those closest to you. Lean into them when you feel too weak.

Take care of yourself, Momma. When the pain becomes too heavy, climb into a bath. Shed the tears you hold back. You suffered a great loss. You deserve to grieve.

Don't carry this weight alone. Find someone to confide in. Whether your confidant is a therapist, your best friend, or someone who shares a story similar to yours, confide in her. Allow her to fill up your cup. You are worthy of it all, Momma.

You are strong.

You. Are. Worthy.

With all of my love,

Madison

Texas

14 False Guilt and Depression

Rhythmic gymnastics was years behind me, yet I felt compelled to demonstrate a *tour jetè* to my friends. I can't even blame this brilliance on alcohol.

A ballet maneuver, a *tour jetè* is essentially a switch kick with pointed toes—and a 180-degree turn. The higher and swifter the kick, the more impressive the movement. Your friend Google can show you how it's performed..

Do not try a *tour jetè* at home.

Anyway, up flew my left foot, up leapt my right foot, with impressive height, I might add. I spun around until . . .

My feet, my thighs, my chest, my chin, my arms, and my hands all crash-landed at the same time. That's right. Total pancake . . . and from such an impressive height.

That's what depression felt like: both legs were swept out from under me and I crashed with incredible force.

Falling flat with my entire body sprawled on the floor didn't knock me out. However, it knocked the air out of me. For some, falling flat knocks them out. They're down for the count.

Even if I walk through a valley as dark as the grave.

I will not be afraid of any danger

because you are with me.

Psalm 23:4.

ERV

If mourning is a black hole, then depression swallows you into a grief vortex. The whirling force deprives you of the energy to crawl out of said deep hole.

Did you know that right behind divorce, the loss of a loved one is the second highest cause of stress, depression, and grief? You never met your loved one, but your child was real. You lost someone you loved.

Jenny admitted, "Still, five months after the loss, smiling felt foreign to my face. I barely survived each day. I just wanted to die—I didn't want to die, I just wanted to cease to exist."

Like a pack of wolves, grief attacked me and pulled me into a wilderness of darkness to die a slow death. I fought off depression with a stick.

Are you fighting depression, or have you succumbed to the wolf pack? Are you as honest with yourself as you need to be?

Phone a friend, if you're—

- prone to depression
- feeling like grief is slurping you into a black hole
- thinking, *I don't care if I emerge from the darkness*
- harboring thoughts of *I don't want to live.*

Set this book down and google counselors in your area. Then call and schedule an appointment.

Needing a doctor doesn't mean you're crazy. Talking through trauma makes you human.

I asked a family friend, Gwenn Garmon M.D., "What would you say to someone who's grieving?"

"Miscarriage is really, really sad. Recognize that you've experienced the death of a loved one. Talk to the people who surround you." Gwenn advised. "If your sadness is getting darker, then talk to a professional. Lows are normal, but if you're stuck in a low, then we have to help you get unstuck."

Please tell me that I'm not the only one who's ever walked in the opposite direction on an escalator. Similarly, existing while depressed requires more effort.

Until I lost my footing, I didn't understand the notion of "ready feet" described in Ephesians 6.

> *"Therefore put on the full armor of God so that when the day of evil comes, you may be able to stand your ground, after you have done everything, to stand. Stand firm then . . . with your feet fitted with the readiness that comes from the gospel of peace,"* Ephesians 6:13–15, NIV.

I thought I understood "ready feet." I picture football players doing quick-feet drills, or boxers shuffling, prancing, ready to pounce.

Here's what finally occurred to me. In two verses, Paul mentions "feet" three times. The goal at the end of the fight? Standing, just standing.

Sometimes, even when I fight like a champion, I still get knocked off my feet. Courage scrambles up again.

After we've fought depression, chased hope, and burned through our emotional cache, our

Good people might fall again and again. but they always get up. Proverbs 24:16. ERV

goal is not to run a marathon. The goal is only to remain standing—with feet fitted in the readiness that comes from the gospel of peace. And if standing requires more labor than you possess, allow me to encourage you with this: Paul doesn't place a timetable on when to stand again.

Slowing down is natural. However, please don't allow your world to screech to a halt. Force yourself to move.

"Are you blaming yourself?" was the first question Lori asked me.

"I'm trying not to."

"Good. Because it wasn't your fault."

Sandie told me, "Sam, the miscarriage wasn't your fault. They have their own romper room in there. There was nothing you could have done."

Before I shook false guilt, I asked Dia, "Did I do something wrong?"

"No, Sam, it wasn't your fault?"

"Am I going to be able to have babies?"

"Of course! You're going to be just fine."

Have you begun playing the "If only" blame-yourself-game yet? Do you wonder: *If only I'd driven to the hospital sooner, the doctor could've prevented my miscarriage or stopped the miscarriage once it started. If only I hadn't drunk so much caffeinated coffee or soda.*

Let's review the facts about pregnancy loss. According to the Mayo Clinic, "miscarriage is the spontaneous loss of a pregnancy before the 20th week. Many miscarriages occur because the fetus isn't developing normally. Problems with the baby's chromosomes are responsible for about 50 percent of early pregnancy loss. Most of these chromosome problems occur by chance as the embryo divides and grows, although it becomes more common as women age. Sometimes a health condition, such as poorly controlled diabetes or a uterine problem, might lead to miscarriage. Often, however, the cause of miscarriage isn't known. About eight to 20 percent of known pregnancies end in miscarriage. Because many women miscarry before they even know that they're pregnant, the total number of actual miscarriages is most likely higher."

I hope your doctor assured you that nothing you did caused the miscarriage. Your baby's death wasn't your fault. You know that, right?

Maybe, through the miscarriage, God protected us from complications beyond our wildest dreams. I don't know. I do know the miscarriage was not your fault. Your friends will tell you the same thing, too. Believe them—they're right.

After my miscarriage I called Grandma. Not only did Grandma experience two miscarriages, she also lost her son John when he was six months old. When she said, "Accept that there might have been something wrong with the baby," I heard the deeper truth: My grandma recited these words to herself repeatedly as she grieved.

My grandparents married December 29, 1944. Two weeks later my grandpa left for Germany. While Grandpa was deployed, Grandma birthed John on September 28, 1945.

Nine months nearly to the day. *You go, Grandpa.*

However, John died in March of 1946 from heart complications, weeks shy of my grandpa's

return from the war. Grandpa never met his first son. Their pain was much like ours.

I pressed the phone to my ear, despising the hundreds of miles between my Grandma and myself. Desperate to hear what she spoke in her soft whisper of a voice, I concentrated on every quiet word.

"John was in bad shape," Grandma told me. "He cried constantly throughout his short, hard life. I remember not having high hopes for his future. Before John's death, and afterward, I just had to trust the Lord and keep going. Now your baby won't suffer the ways of this wicked world. You'll see him again one day."

As often as you try to convince your head that the miscarriage wasn't your fault, acceptance within your heart may remain another matter entirely.

Overcoming guilt is that infamous eighteen-inch journey—the longest distance on earth—from your head to your heart. You're not alone in your fears, doubts, and questions.

You're normal. Broken hearts aren't mended with the snap of a finger.

I constantly reminded myself: It's not my fault. There's nothing I could have done differently. If you're like me, I needed reassurance from several friends.

Do you struggle with false guilt and wonder, *Why did this happen to me?* From a medical perspective, it's important to understand that our bodies recognize when a baby may not survive inside or outside the womb and miscarriage is the result.

If you need reassurance that your miscarriage was not your fault, ask as often as necessary to receive this scripted answer: "It's not your fault."

Praying to God is not always about asking for an explanation or solution. Prayer reveals our faith in God who cares enough to listen. When we feel that hope died and lies beyond our grasp, it's crucial to believe in God and in the hope of life after death.

Grief is sadness with hope, but depression is sadness without hope. God embedded eternity in our hearts. Hope never slumbers. Hope remains awake, waiting for us to catch a glimpse of hope's eternal light. Hope alive awaits outside our heart's door for the fog of mourning blindness to clear.

Please don't let your world stop. Force yourself to keep moving, even if it's only one small step.

As Lona said, "Keep going. One foot in front of the other."

Reassess and reassure yourself. You don't need to punish yourself for your miscarriage. Stop flogging yourself with blame and guilt.

Review the facts: Your miscarriage *is not* your fault.

As Lona said,
"Keep going.
One foot in front
of the other."

Reflection: What's On My Heart?

Lies I Tell Myself
What false guilt still plagues me? On a sheet of paper, list the lies you repeat. Renew your mind, beside each lie write the truth: "It's not my fault."

Friends don't let friends stay depressed. If you're depressed, who will you call to hold you accountable to take the steps you need to obtain the help you need?

Call a friend who will hold me accountable:
Name of friend:
Phone number:
Date, time, and place for meeting:

Here are some harder questions. Have you talked to a counselor yet?

Did you schedule an appointment like Sam recommended?

Did you take your medication?

Did you locate a counselor? Oh, I'm sorry. Did you think I was kidding? Did you think I wouldn't know?

Counseling Center Phone Number:
Name of Counselor I'm scheduled to see:
Date and time of appointment:
Address of counseling center:

A Beautiful This

The surge of a 10-story tsunami
Crescendos behind me.
My heels slip on shifting sand.
I dig in for purchase, acquiring no traction.
The beast bears down upon the barrier reef
The overwhelming, all-consuming, intoxicating Grief.
I spare no frantic glance.
Water droplets pelt my back. I am going to drown.
The wave buries me whole.
Alive? But how?
I am tossed, thrown
Buffeted by riptide and tow
Sense of direction, gone
Lost forever, my will to press on.
Dissolved plans and purpose.
I possess no more control than storm-throttled grasses
Save a single spark.
Determination? Hope?
I dare not define this fragile ember
A withered leaf clinging to summer with an unsteady tremor.
My shoulder slams against an unknown force.
My limbs ricochet from mass to mass without course.
My head is wrenched from side to side
Drenched hair whips across my eyes
Current propels me down to the depths.
I clutch an object within my battered fist
I recall not its name, despite the din
This piece is valuable.

I know deep within
I tighten my grip on the unknown.
My world rages. I am alone.
Who am I? Where am I?
My stomach lurches with questions.
Elusive answers in a state of transmutation.
The wave swells.
Squeezes. Pummels.
Coalesced pressure against my soul.
The deafening roars grow.
I cringe, desperate to escape the beast
My free hand encompasses my curled fingers.
I sacrifice for the unknown treasure,
I will not survive this.
Grief growls. Wolves cornering their prey.
I cower.
Thunder crashes. Rumblings echo.
Streaks of lightening take hold. I begin to fray.
Not death, but
Silence.
Absolute stillness.
I float weightless and inventory
I am changed, but I am still me.
Not dragged to the depths as I originally believed
But thrown to the sky, to the birthplace of dreams
Starlight illuminates my metamorphosis.
Grief transformed me into a beautiful this.
The past is gone but not forgotten.
The next choice is mine and no one else's.
I release a hand and uncurl my grasp
The spark will ignite and . . .

Reflection: What's On My Heart?

Finish the last line of the poem. What happens? What do you look like? Your answer doesn't have to rhyme with grasp.

What choices will you make on the other side of your grief?

In the Words of Others

Dear Normal Mom,

I stared at the double pink line, dropped my head and uttered a four-letter curse. No, no, no. This cannot be happening.

My son was only seven months old. I'd not forgotten the nausea, swollen legs, and heartburn. I heard women say, "Oh, I just loved being pregnant!"

Are you even from this planet? Pregnancy, right? Aren't we both talking about another human taking over our bodies for nine months?

I gained an obscene amount of weight. I now have stretch marks from my knees to my nipples, and my wackado hormones turned me into a psycho.

Then came the postpartum depression that nearly destroyed my marriage. One night, I white knuckled the crib, half out of my mind, and shouted at my newborn, "Just sleep! Why won't you sleep!" This is why mother's shake their children. They just want the sound to stop.

My husband tore into the nursery to find a wailing child in the crib, and a sobbing woman crumpled on the floor.

So, no. I didn't experience any joy when I took a positive pregnancy test. Only dread. I can't do this again!

Maybe you're in college. Maybe you're unmarried. Maybe you were raped. Maybe you just can't handle being pregnant and the life change a new life implies.

If you were relieved you miscarried, you're not alone. You're not crazy. There is no judgement here, only love.

XOXOX,
A Mom Who's Been There

15 Embracing Hope in the Midst of Mourning

I stared vacantly out my office window. Mourning's static in my brain made listening difficult. A friend's advice meant to help buzzed around me like a fly.

Despite the vast number of her words of encouragement, the only words that penetrated were, "Cling to Jesus."

Before you think, *Wow, how profound*, here's how my brain reacted. My mind conjured an image of me as the woman in the New Testament who suffered with the vaginal flow of blood. Her 12-year struggle compelled her to push through the crowd with hope to reach out in faith to touch Jesus' cloak to receive healing. (Luke 8:42–44)

Only, my story didn't play out the same way as that woman healed by Jesus' power. When I reached for Jesus' cloak, the fabric slipped through my fingers as Jesus strode away toward the next town.

I'm gonna miss him!

Desperation coursed through me, igniting a burst of energy. I lunged and with all my strength I clasped Jesus' cloak. Jesus didn't notice me!

My elusive Hope accelerated as fast as a motorboat ferrying a tuber.

I tightened my grip.

Cling to Jesus.

Cling to Jesus.

Cling to Jesus.

I bounced along the road behind Him, dirt and pebbles flying in our wake.

I'm ridiculous. Encouraging you to hope when I'm so grief-stricken that hope feels nearly as possible as catching Santa Claus filling a stocking.

How do I write about hope when devastation and disappointment crushes me? Hope slips through my fingers like sand and water. Yet, minuscule grains of damp sand and salty hope stuck to my fingers and psyche.

This book needs to talk about hope.

Hope . . .

I typed that word, then wrote a bunch of fluffy nonsense.

I gagged, then hit Ctrl+A and deleted the entire page.

I re-typed the word "hope" at the top of the page, leaned back in my chair and dove into a bag of Nacho Cheese Doritos and stared at a blank computer screen.

This book needs to talk about hope.

More staring.

More munching and crunching.

I swiveled my chair from side to side.

I'm empty. I've got nothing.

My eyebrows dove downward.

Orange fingers plunged into the red bag.

More tooth-rattling crunches shattered the silence.

"Jesus. I'm a bit jaded as of late on this hope topic. If you want any hope in our story, you best get crackin'."

The result of that "prayer" and the words I typed surprised even me.

Oh, Snap!

One December 23rd, I found myself in a hopeless situation. Snow drifts blanketed the Minnesota landscape. Trekking from the Twin Cities to Chicago, I left from a different part of the Cities than usual and drove on a less familiar road than my normal route. Green road signs sported a fluffy, white coat—just like everything else in the state.

My left windshield wiper quit working. Despite the sub-zero temps, I rolled down the window and manually forced the wiper up and down to clear away fast-falling snow. Every few minutes I rolled up my window to thaw before repeating the process.

The air rushing in bothered my contacts. I rubbed my eye with such intensity, one contact lens popped out and landed who-knows-where. My good eye squinted through a snow-challenged windshield. I glanced between my map and the snow-covered road signs.

Ten months since I've seen my family. I can survive 375 miles to sweet home Chicago. I can do this.

My tires slicked across a transparent patch of black ice. I yanked my foot from the gas pedal and counteracted the steering wheel with the direction of the car.

The car swooped from one lane to the other. The back end spun out. I skidded into a ditch,

facing non-existent, oncoming traffic. My heart thundered as I emerged from the car to assess my situation. The tops of cattails poked through snowdrifts surrounding my vehicle.

My heart and hope sunk like my boots buried in the snow bank.

Outlook? Not good.

My 360-view of frosted farmland revealed acres and miles of soft deep snow, proving that no human life was within my scope.

I stared at the phone in my hand. "Who should I call?"

No bars.

"Ha. Can't call."

My mittened hand braced my face. *Situations like this actually happen in real life? I need help and I can't even call anyone.*

How about Me?

"Uh! Okay, God. You'll do." But I harbored doubts. I climbed into the driver's seat, tossed my cell phone atop the map in the passenger seat, grabbed the steering wheel, and prayed with Oscar-award-winning enthusiasm, "God, please help me get out of this ditch."

I sighed and switched to reverse. I backed up several feet, threw the gear shift into drive, then eased the car back onto the road. Performing a three-point turn, I parked my car on the shoulder and blinked.

Did that just happen?

I opened the driver-side door. My boots crunched as I circled the car. Then I peered into the ditch to survey the imprint left by my car.

Yep! Really happened. Yep! God just

answered my prayer with the snap of His finger. There's no other explanation.

"Thanks, God."

My hopeless-to-me and stuck-in-a-ditch circumstances reminded me: I'm loved and heard by God—who specializes in hope. His power dragged me out of the quicksand, or 'quicksnow'.

After my pregnancy loss, drifts of mourning overwhelmed me. The emotional blizzard of miscarriage left me stuck in a depressing ditch surrounded by an emotional landscape of hopelessness.

Tears wept over my present despair drowned my past elation, quashing all joy of discovering life in my womb. Lamentations is traditionally attributed to the authorship of the prophet Jeremiah. Nicknamed "the weeping prophet," his words read like a poetic journal entry of my suffering.

> *586 to 575 BCE: I am the man who has seen the afflictions that come from the rod of God's wrath. He has brought me into deepest darkness, shutting out all light. He has turned against me. Day and night His hand is heavy on me. He has made me old and has broken my bones.*
>
> *He has built forts against me and surrounded me with anguish and distress. He buried me in dark places, like those long dead. He has walled me in; I cannot escape; He has fastened me with heavy chains. And though I cry and shout, He will not hear my*

prayers! He has shut me into a place of high, smooth walls; He has filled my path with detours.

He lurks like a bear, like a lion, waiting to attack me. He has dragged me into the underbrush and torn me with His claws, leaving me bleeding and desolate. He has bent His bow and aimed it squarely at me, and sent His arrows deep within my heart.

I have become a joke to all my people. All day long they sing songs about me and make fun of me. He has filled me with bitterness and given me a cup of deepest sorrows to drink. He has made me eat gravel and broken my teeth; He has rolled me in ashes and dirt.

I thought I would never have peace again. I forgot about good things. I said to myself, "I no longer have any hope that the Lord will help me."

Remember, I am very sad, and I have no home. Remember the bitter poison that You gave me. I remember well all my troubles, and I am very sad. Lamentations 3:1–16, TLB; 3:14,17–20, ERV.

The depth of my mourning related to Jeremiah's heart-wrenching lament. I felt spited. Can you relate?

I grew up hearing in church, "God loves you, God loves you, God loves you." If God truly loved me, how could He let this happen? I believed God could have saved my baby, but He didn't.

I forgot about all the good things He did in my life. I forgot about His divine oath to:

> *"show up and take care of you as I promised . . . I have plans to take care of you . . . plans to give you the future you hope for,"* Jeremiah 29:11, MSG.

In Jeremiah 31:14–15, MSG, Jeremiah's words offered some perspective regarding adversity in life.

> *Verse 14: "'And my people will be filled and satisfied with the good things I give them.' This message is from the Lord."*
>
> *Verse 15: "This is what the Lord says: 'A sound is heard in Ramah bitter crying and great sadness Rachel cries for her children, and she refuses to be comforted, because her children are gone.'"*

Verse 14 mirrored my desire to be pregnant. In sharp contrast, verse 15 described my melancholy and despair over the death of my child. When my womb was filled with a growing child, I was satisfied—happy. Then boom! My child was gone, leaving me devastated. Jeremiah described my before, my present, and the loss of the future to parent my child.

Following Jeremiah's description of Rachel weeping for her children, God reaffirmed His divine promise:

> *"This is what the LORD says:*

'Restrain your voice from weeping and your eyes from tears, for your work will be rewarded' declares the LORD. '. . . there is hope for your future,'"
Jeremiah 31:16–17, NIV.

Skeptically, I thought, *Okay. God, we'll see about that. Show me whatcha got.*

Hope Escaped

After Jesus' birth, Matthew 2:18 referred again to Rachel's weeping and great mourning. Scholars from the East approached King Herod and asked, "Where can we find the newborn King of the Jews?"

The wise men's question and the threat of a newborn king terrified Herod. Paranoid, yet thorough, Herod demanded the slaughter of every Jewish boy under the age of two.

Herod's slaughter of innocent infants in Bethlehem reawakened Rachel's grief. Rachel embodied mothers' tears and intense mourning for children no longer in the land of the living.

Imagine a city ten or twelve miles from where you live. Ramah was six miles northwest of Jerusalem and ten to twelve miles from Bethlehem, where Rachel was buried. Jeremiah describes the mothers' anguish so severe that their wailing was heard over ten miles away! Like us, a hideous emotional darkness fell over those mothers. How on earth are we supposed to survive this crushing pain?

Victory by Knock Out

Was God aware of Rachel's pain? Absolutely. God's plan to restore hope was already in progress.

An angel gave Joseph, Jesus' earthly father, a heads-up to flee from Bethlehem with his small family. Hope escaped Herod's wrath and fled to Egypt, carried in the arms of his parents. After Herod died, Jesus' family returned to Israel.

God also experienced Rachel's pain when He sacrificed His only Son to be our hope. The only way to save us from hopeless separation from God—the permanent death penalty for our sin— was for God's Son to stretch out His arms to the East and the West and bridge the gap between man and God.

Friday always comes before Sunday.

On Friday, when Jesus hung on that dirty, splintered cross, He didn't appear glorious. Our future didn't look too bright either. Hope died tacked to a tree. To the world, His death meant *Game Over*. So much for Hope escaping.

Here's the catch: Like an older sibling who intentionally loses in a game of tag, Jesus allowed death to catch Him.

Jesus knew Sunday was a comin'.

And Hope didn't just escape death. Hope punched death square in the mouth.

The Comfort of Hope

Hope maneuvers us out of snowy ditches. Hope rebuilds broken dreams. Hope rewrites our stories. Hope redeems our present suffering for a future good. Hope provides courage to endure life's trials and heartaches. Hope restores. Hope promises a reunion with our children for eternity.

As I thought about my baby's journey home to heaven, two verses in Hebrews 11:13; 38, NABRE echoed in my head.

"They were aliens and strangers on earth . . . the world was not worthy of them."

I was intrigued by the thought that earth was not worthy of the unborn child I lost. My child skipped the gunk of life and earned a Fast Pass straight into Jesus' presence. Hope that rested on my faith linked me to eternity and to the comfort of a reunion with my child, who rests in God's loving presence.

Have You Ever Said?

"There has to be something better than this life?" That's hope. If you believe the answer to your heart's desire is heaven, then you possess faith.

Heaven, great, right? So the best hope we have is death? I was 100% invested in becoming a mother. Miscarriage laid siege to my heart and set my future on fire. I didn't know if the flame came from outside or within. I longed to escape. Yet, Scripture provided glimmers of hope.

Because I was so empty and out of ideas, I searched Scripture for hope. Matthew 12:2, NIV presented a clear choice regarding hope:

"In his name the nations will put their hope."

Two options faced me: I could figure out hope and peace on my own, or choose to trust God's Son. He battled death and won and was strong enough to hold me together and to heal my broken heart.

My emotional pain crushed me. *How will I survive this?* Mourning narrowed my emotional peripheral vision. Grief caused me to hyper-focus on the devastation of the loss. At my breaking point, my heart wailed in pain. Turning my faith to God's promises required concerted effort.

On a rifle, the sight is a cross in the middle of the scope. To aim at a target, one focuses on the centerpoint of the crosshairs. Mourning points to a temporal hope, not a biblical hope. When overwhelming emotions line-up the glum-dum-ho-hum side of life, that's all we feel.

In the deepest valley of grief, losing sight of hope can be normal. Staying stuck, though, presents emotional, spiritual, and physical problems. When despair remains the focal point for too long, endurance and strength arise from the wellspring of hope and our trust in God. Hope doesn't deny the loss. Hope acknowledges loss while whispering the story of survival.

What's the difference between a natural, worldly hope and the gift of spiritual hope?

- **Temperal hope** aligns our focus on our wishes, expectations, presumptions, and personal goals. It fixates our hopes on immediate gratification or worldly satisfaction.

- **Spiritual hope**—a gift from the God of comfort and compassion—is a deeper understanding of a future that looks beyond our current circumstances. Spiritual hope trusts God's character, as well as God's work, on our behalf behind the 'seens' in the midst of our suffering.

Presumption anticipates gratification. Temporal hope, fueled by emotions, breeds

As a friend said, "Right now, I don't care about heaven. I just need to know how to get through today."

helplessness. Despair revolts against a quiet trust that waits on God's promises. Never measure hope by disappointment or dashed expectations. God's unlimited power is stronger than our expectations and our fears.

Defeat shatters temporal dreams. And for some, desperation also shatters their faith, turning them against hope in God.

Temporal hope ebbs and flows, like the tide of an emotional tsunami of disappointment, depression, despair, and destruction.

What a contrast to the bedrock of biblical hope that exchanges courage and strength for weakness and exhaustion. What a contrast that promises a future and the unseen miracle that God revives our hurting heart when we cultivate our trust in Him.

In times of crisis, our brains are wired to brood on misery. Did you know that speaking a story of hope and gratitude overrides the negative wiring of our brains?

I know this sounds absurd, but, in the depth of your despair, try to cultivate consistent gratitude.

Some people white-knuckle bitterness so long that despondency settles into a comfortable habit. Courageous hope patiently endures pain with a grateful heart.

How did Jeremiah defy hardship and heartache to override his brain chemistry and negative thoughts? Let's take another look at a page from Jeremiah's journal that reflects his habit of hope:

> *"But this I call to mind, and therefore I have hope: The steadfast love of the*

LORD never ceases; his mercies never come to an end; they are new every morning; great is your faithfulness. 'The LORD is my portion,' says my soul, 'therefore I will hope in him.' The LORD is good to those who wait for him, to the soul who seeks him. It is good that one should wait quietly for the salvation of the LORD.

"Let him sit alone in silence when it is laid on him; let him put his mouth in the dust—there may yet be hope; For the Lord will not cast off forever, but, though he cause grief, he will have compassion according to the abundance of his steadfast love for he does not afflict from his heart or grieve the children of men," Lamentations 3:21–26, 28–29, 31–33, ESV.

Even as pain throbs like a heartbeat, only one hope exists deeper than my loss—the truth of God's character and the truth that God loves and hears and sees me.

This is a truth that you and I must face together. I've not declared false promises to you yet, and I've no intention to start now.

Tears slide down my face as I type this: We may never bear children, or more children, as the case may be. I find it's impossible not to hope to have children in my future, but I don't own a crystal ball.

The story of hope is not one of enlarging our family, but that God can restore our hearts, and make us whole again.

Remember your promise to me.

It gives me hope.

You comfort me in my suffering.

because your promise gives me new life.

Psalm 119:49-50.
ERV

With faith, I now approach heaven. With hope I plead for relief. Love embodied in Jesus kneels beside me. Hope loosens the grip of grief.

How about you? With hope you will be comforted. With hope you will be joyful again. Have faith the Lord will guide you to this Hope.

Adjust your sights on the promises of the Lord. I'll take my cue from Jeremiah. In the midst of his grief, Jeremiah kept his sights on the worthiness of God.

> *The LORD is good to those whose hope is in Him; to the one who seeks Him; it's good to wait quietly for the salvation of the LORD. It's good for a woman to bear the yoke while she is young. Let her sit alone in silence for the LORD has laid it on her. Let her bury her face in the dust—there may yet be hope.*
>
> *For men and women are not cast off by the LORD forever. Though He brings grief, He will show compassion, so great is His unfailing love. For He does not willingly bring affliction or grief to the children of men . . .*
>
> *I called on Your Name, O LORD, from the depths of the pit. You heard my plea: 'Do not close Your ears to my cry for relief.' You came near when I called you and you said, 'Do not fear.' O LORD, you took up my case. You redeemed my life. You have seen, O LORD, the wrong done to me. Uphold*

my cause," Lamentations 3:21–33, 55–59, NIV.

Jeremiah ranted to God, zoomed in on his grief. He vented to the LORD—legitimate, illogical, unreasonable, loud, painful, and relieving. The act of hope vents sorrow, despair, and sadness to God.

Jeremiah vents. Check. He accuses God of *"bringing him into darkness without any light."* (Lamentations 3:2). Right there with you, Jer.

Then the habit of his mind and heart recalls:

> *" . . . the steadfast love of the LORD*
> *never ceases. His mercies never come*
> *to an end,"* Lamentations 3:22–23, ESV.

Wait. What? Rewind. A profound change occurs as Jeremiah writes. It is the same change— the strikeout—I noticed when LeAnna showed me her journal entry:

> *Today was our little one's due date. I feel like there is always something to remind me that we lost a baby. I just remember when we started trying for a baby, how excited we were. Then when we found out when it was happening, we had so much joy last summer! It seems like yesterday, but it also seems so far away that joy can't be recaptured. I know that happiness is a choice, but right now it just seems like there is ~~nothing~~ not much to be thankful for.*

In LeAnna's pain, her feelings that there was "~~nothing~~" to be thankful for clashed with the truth she knew: "God is still at work in my life."

When Jeremiah realigned his sights on the LORD, he saw the truth. *"Yet,"* Jeremiah said, *"My God is faithful. He has a never-ending compassion. He is my hope and my portion."*

With eyes still fixed on our Heavenly Father, Jeremiah took a deep breath, maybe several.

> *Let him sit alone [in hope] and keep quiet, because God has laid it on him [for his benefit],* Lamentations 3:26, AMP.

In the silence, in the stillness, God drew near to Jeremiah. God restored peace to the weeping prophet's heart and the pain subsided. When it flared again, God pulled Jeremiah through the same process. Jeremiah acknowledged that God heard his cry and saw his pain. When God restored Jeremiah's perspective, then Jeremiah boldly sought the LORD to uphold his cause.

When we clench our interpretations of God's blessings, we don't leave room for His work. Jeremiah wrote in Lamentation 3:27, MSG:

> *"It's a good thing when you're young to stick it out through the hard times."*

What we learn about mourning and hope from miscarriage strengthens us and provides wisdom when we experience inevitable trials and heartbreaks in the future. Temperal hope can't guarantee a fulfillment of our wishes and personal goals. Our presumptions about our future may not match God's plans. Accepting this difficult truth moves us into a place of freedom.

Freedom to be healed. Freedom to move through this present mourning. Freedom to receive joy from a future that does not look the way we envisioned.

No one claims that moving through brokenness is easy. When I heard the poem written by Loretta Burns, I instantly memorized it. I love the simplistic description of our tug-of-war with God.

> *As children bring their broken toys,*
> *with tears, for us to mend,*
> *I brought my broken dreams to God*
> *Because He was my friend.*
> *But then instead of leaving Him*
> *in peace to work alone,*
> *I hung around and tried to help*
> *with ways that were my own.*
> *At last I snatched them back and cried,*
> *"How can You be so slow?!"*
> *"My child," He said, "What could I do?*
> *You never let them go."*

God still waits on standby . . . waiting for your sight-aligned requests. Like Jeremiah, have you:

- vented?
- fixed your sights on the faithfulness, majesty, and mercy of God?
- realized the endless possibilities of gifts coming from God's self-giving character with which that He longs to delight you?
- waited in silence and sensed His presence at your side?
- embraced God's unconditional love of you?
- asked God to fight for you, to fulfill your hopes?

Reflection: What's On My Heart?

Line Up Your Cross-Hairs and Let Go: Sam, I'm ready to practice the habit of hope and gratitude. Here's my hope-filled list.

1.

2

3

4

5

6

7

8

9

10.

In the Words of Others

Dear Mamma,

"I ask you, therefore, not to be discouraged . . . . For this reason . . . I kneel before the Father, from whom His whole family in heaven and on earth derives its name. I pray that out of His glorious riches He may strengthen you with power through His Spirit in your inner being so that Christ may dwell in your hearts through faith.

And I pray that you, being rooted and established in love, may have power, together with all the Lord's holy people, to grasp how wide and long and high and deep is the love of Christ, and to know this love that surpasses knowledge—that you may be filled to the measure of the fullness of God.

Now to Him who is able to do immeasurably more than we ask or imagine, according to His power that is at work within us, to Him be the glory in the church and in Christ Jesus throughout all generations forever and ever. Amen." Ephesians 3:13–20, NIV.

Love, Sam

In the Words of Others

Dear Precious, Broken Hearts,

Faith weeps. I've experienced miscarriage, divorce, and the death of my 29-year-old son. With each loss, all sense of hope and my God-given identity and calling vanished. My unexpected tragedies tested my loyalty to God. My quandary became: Will I allow God to enter the shattering emptiness of my brokenness?

It's one thing to say, "I trust God," and another to entrust a beloved child into God's presence for eternity. Yet, the volcanics of my suffering gave rise to a faith that erupted from my broken hallelujah.

One Sunday, my pastor asked fellow grievers to divulge thoughts about the 'object' of our future hopes. Our answers were to flow from Colossians 3:1;5, NIV: "Set your hearts on things above, not earthly things" and "faith and love springs from the hope that's stored up for us in heaven." The pastor instructed us to share our "hopes" with each other. Wishful hopes tumbled from my table-mates' mouths:

- find a spouse, marry, buy a house, and start a family
- build and advance in a successful career.

Worthy, normal desires, right? Yet every shape-shifting hope they shared? Crushable. Perishable. Finite. Temporary. Perhaps unattainable, or beyond human control. Success or failure of their hopes required the cooperation and favor of circumstances, people, even the economy. Their answers jarred my insides. Out of step with those sitting at that table, I squirmed as I shared my "hope list" born from my painful life losses.

- allow myself to mourn
- comfort others mourning a traumatic loss
- offer hope to the hopeless and helpless
- walk through every door God opens.

After being informed that my firstborn was killed in Afghanistan, my heart thumped at these oddly comforting words, "God numbers our days." (Psalms 139:16) Was I happy with the number of days God allotted to my children? Nope. I engaged in some frank, in-your-face conversations with God. When the pulse of my children's fleeting, earthly bodies stopped, all affliction vanished, they entered into the joy of the Lord, which comforts my mother's heart. War, death, sorrow, crying, sickness, mourning, sin, or pain can never assault my children ever again.

The true essence of who my children are now dwell alive and secure in the Hope of heaven. Our children's short-lived lives carved their love and legacy upon our hearts. Two days belong to God—the day God planned our birth and the date God knows we'll die. Between those two dates is one simple line—the-dash-in-between—that stands for time that's yours and mine.

To encourage others losing their battles of hope and faith, I want my 'dash in-between' to reveal God-infused resilience and a relentless faith in the hope of the Lifegiver.

When breath leaves my body and my two precious children embrace me and shout "Mom," I long to stand before the Lamb of God with them and hear, "Well done, good and faithful servant. Enter into the joy of your Lord," Matthew 25:21, NKJV.

Scoti

Colorado

16 Infertility: Maternal Limbo Land

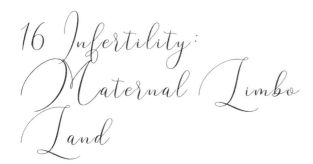

To outward appearances, Mike and Jan were the perfect couple who had everything—financial security, a beautiful home, status in their community, a strong church family, beloved by in-laws, and a solid marriage until . . .

Jan was diagnosed with chlamydia. After a number of years of trying to conceive a child, they both opted to see an infertility professional. Mike's sperm weren't swimmers, and his sperm also displayed damage caused by chlamydia.

Sexually active before marriage, neither one realized they were infected and neither one received treatment for chlamydia. For Jan, not receiving treatment proved overwhelming. Even though she displayed no symptoms, chlamydia damaged her reproductive system, leaving her infertile.

Incapable of conceiving a child, Mike and Jan's marriage failed. The pain and shame of the consequences of chlamydia, a sexually transmitted disease, caused Jan to withdraw from close friends. Mike and Jan divorced. She moved to another state, and disappeared.

With the help of antibiotics, Mike escaped the death-of-dreams diagnosis that Jan received. Mike remarried, conceived a child with his new wife, and doted on his daughter.

Chloe and Matt's marriage was also solid. When they failed to conceive, they began in vitro fertilization (IVF). Withdrawing eggs was painful for Chloe, and Matt was embarrassed donating his sperm. Scheduling sex strained their marriage.

After spending tens of thousands of dollars on multiple rounds of treatment, they faced one last shot to conceive. The failure of that last-ditch infertility treatment devastated Chloe.

Emotionally and financially depleted, their marriage survived. Chloe attended a support group and was transparent with friends and co-workers. Her transparency provided a lesson in resolve and courage to those who empathized and lacked any point of reference to understand her struggles.

No matter the cause of infertility or sterility, yearning for biological motherhood makes you the odd man out of the 'Has Kids Club.' With each friend, who announces their pregnancy, the vanishing act of another friendship begins.

After embarking on years of treatment with no success in sight, you wish you could be happy for family and friends who become pregnant. But you're exhausted and your future faces more failed tests and rounds of IVF.

The pain is so great, many delete their social media accounts. Some follow blogs written by women struggling with infertility.

From reading scientific studies, to learning acronyms you never knew existed, to completing IVF, what challenging questions cycle and recycle through your heart and mind as this life crisis confronts you?

- Why me?
- I feel so alone.
- What's wrong with me?
- How is this even possible?
- Why did she get pregnant, and not me?
- What if my treatments don't work?
- How do I decide when to stop treatment?
- Will I ever get pregnant?
- What about surrogacy?
- What if I never have a child?
- Should we adopt?
- Has God heard my prayers?
- Why won't God give me a baby?

Are you tired of the annoying, none-of-their-business question: "When are you going to have a baby?" Don't they understand that you're hanging on for dear life to the roller coaster ride of loneliness, frustration, and hope?

Women struggling with infertility face the battle of the psychosocial stress of infertility, which is both internal—the desire to birth a child—and external—not living up to the expectations of cultural norms. The distress of infertility wounds both the heart and mind.

A friend's 'oops' prego announcement shatters you. How can the 'fertiles' take conceiving a child for granted? And of course, as the one struggling with infertility, you're the last to hear the latest "I'm pregnant!" news.

Caught in the crossfire between scientific, social, ethical, and political rhetoric, or making deal after deal with God, each couple dealing with

infertility must decide how to move forward and choose what they believe is best for their lives.

You may decide on a medical approach that bothers others unenlightened about the agonies of infertility and the soul-searching behind complex choices. One couple, who pursued IVF, did not expect the painful blowback from an upset parent, who held a strong belief that IVF was wrong. The successful IVF treatment resulting in the birth of a child about-faced that grandparent's prior judgment.

Even if you're angry with God, ask for His peace and guidance in your decision making. After you and your husband or partner elect to proceed, set an emotional boundary with those who believe their viewpoint superior to yours. Or those who impose their emotional conflict with a medical procedure upon you.

Melanie Dale, who dealt with infertility, says this in her book *infreakinfertility*: "I realized that God is in that test tube just as sure as God is knitting a fetus together in the womb. Sure, we can put sperm and eggs together just like Fertiles do when they copulate, but only God can make them into an embryo. Only God can make it viable. Only God can make it grow into life."

Wait? How Much Longer?

The wait and weight of infertility and IVF, plus the seesaw of hope and disappointment, ramps up physical and emotional stress. The deep suffering of being childless without consent and living in maternal limbo land is fraught with sadness and grief.

A study conducted with women in IVF treatment revealed "the negative relationships between gratitude and infertility-related stress were explained by a general sense of meaningfulness and acceptance of life.

Women who scored higher on a gratitude questionnaire also reported lower levels of fertility-related stress." Gratitude protected those women from losing hope and meaning for life.

Infertility and IVF ramps up emotional and psychological stress. Henri Nouwen observed:

"Resentment and gratitude cannot coexist, since resentment blocks the perception and experience of life as a gift. My resentment tells me that I don't receive what I deserve. It always manifests itself in envy."

The negative impact of the destructive emotion of envy leads to anxiety, anger, depression, stress, resentment, unhappiness, and being overwhelmed. You're not alone in your struggle.

Fight for hope and purpose in your life outside of your fertility journey. Focus on the favors or gifts God has given you to lighten the emotional heaviness of infertility.

To all who mourn God will give:

beauty for ashes;
joy instead of mourning;
praise instead of heaviness.

For God has planted them like strong and graceful oaks for his own glory.

Isaiah 61:3

ERV

Reflection: What's On My Heart?

Pursue gratitude. Before God formed you in your mother's womb and before you saw the light of day, God prepared holy plans for you. Start a gratitude journal to reflect on the good gifts God gave you.

List five ways God has blessed you.

You are not alone and infertility is not your fault. The following resource written by Melanie Dale, who felt like a babyless freak, wrote a book just for you.

infreakinfertility: How to Survive When Getting Pregnant Gets Hard shares Melanie's raw and real personal journey with infertility, validating the confusing feelings of the fertility-challenged. Written with compassion, humor, and her husband's insights, she unveils the insanity of what happens and gives you tools to keep plodding forward, one step at a time.

In the Words of Others

Dear Sweet Woman,

I'm infertile, too. Ten years, countless doctor visits and various procedures later, I still hoped and hoped and hoped for a child—until the moment the radiologist said, "Birth children are not in your future. Have a nice day."

Stark. Simple. Unfeeling. His words devastated my husband and me. Through blurred vision and heaving sobs, we managed our way toward the exit.

Just then, a friend strolled in, glorious with joy—and obviously pregnant. Why, God? Why does she get to be pregnant? Why can't I have a bio kid? Why am I broken?

I wept, because of the soul-tearing grief. You've felt that pain, too. A couple months later, we brushed off our hands and sought adoption. You may be in a place where these words sound trite to you, but my husband and I both sensed God saying, "I see your desire. It's just not going to look the way you imagined."

Don't give up on your deep, gut-wrenching hope for family. God has a place for you—just as you are.

Our son was conceived out of rape. Our son needed us as much as we needed him. I say this, not flippantly, but as someone who aches as you do: Trust God's plan. Trust.

I pray for you this day. That you will find hope. That you will know joy. You are worthy of love.

Love Always,

One of Your Tribe

17 Bev's Story: Adoption Godsend

"Mom, I think something's wrong with me. I don't think I'll be able to have babies."

"Oh, don't be so dramatic, Beverly. You've only been married a couple months."

I rolled my eyes and swallowed my sarcasm. *Not every woman is a baby-making factory that produces children like it's an annual tradition.*

I wanted to believe my mom. However, deep down I suspected something wasn't right. For one thing, sex hurt. And despite what other people said, the pain wasn't caused by the position or my being "too tight." I knew better.

After two years of regular, unprotected sex, we still weren't pregnant. I finally scheduled a doctor's visit to ask some questions.

"Pelvic Inflammatory Disease," my doctor diagnosed. "I'm sorry, Bev. It's highly unlikely that you'll ever carry your own child. Miracles happen all the time though, don't they?"

Miracles happen, yes, I have faith. Even so, I'm also a pragmatist.

If my husband and I tried another two years and then put our names on the waiting list for adoption, the wait would be even longer.

I held out an open hand for the hope of a miracle. With my other hand, I signed on the dotted line, placing our names on the adoption agency's years-long waiting list.

Every month I prayed for the miracle that didn't happen. Every month I prayed for a call from the adoption agency that never came.

Throughout the next couple of years, doctors performed several different procedures. Nothing worked. Doctors echoed what my doctor already forecasted, "It's highly unlikely you will ever carry your own child."

But miracles happen, right? Each month my menstrual cycle arrived like clockwork. Each period felt like a death and I sobbed until my abdomen ached from heaving.

That's it. I'm gonna fix this.

I purchased every book on pregnancy and infertility I could lay my hands on. I bought pens with different-colored ink, highlighters, post-its, three different brands of thermometers, and a scroll of paper that gave the Bible a run for Scripture's money.

This is gonna work. My sex graph looked like a geometry final, and a constellation chart made a baby.

Month one, we laughed about the idiocy of essentially engaging in sex when a timer hummed, but intercourse was still fun. A couple months in, my husband would be exhausted from work, or outside performing maintenance on machinery and I'd nag him into the bedroom. "Hurry, honey, come on! We've gotta do this right now!" Sex was as sexy as tightening a bolt on a carburetor.

Despite all my efforts, every month my period dropped in and taunted me. I battled depression. Not one menses passed that I didn't weep myself to sleep.

All my friends got pregnant with the effort required to blink. Their beautiful, round bellies protected the babies their husbands placed in them. Then their arms cradled child after child while their families increased the way I'd expected my family to grow.

Then when I sobbed during sex, my husband drew the line, "That's enough, Sweetheart. We can't keep doing this."

I know he's right.

After five years of fruitless effort to get pregnant, doctors performed a hysterectomy. The hysterectomy was one of the best decisions I ever made. With no hope left to ever become pregnant, I no longer had a period to remind me of my infertility. The grief assaulting me month after month finally abated. The hurt didn't disappear, but the pain decreased.

At that time, my husband and I both worked for the Air Force. I worked in the JAG office as a civilian, and he performed maintenance on helicopters.

Out of the Wild Blue Wonder

One Friday morning a woman called me at work. "Hello, Bev? This is Jill from the adoption agency. You're going to have a son."

The breath vanished from my lungs. I lost my ability to breathe all together. I attempted words. I couldn't vocalize a sound. An eruption of tears

cascaded down my cheeks. The overflow obscured my vision and my hearing deafened.

I failed to notice the airmen and military personnel who stopped and stared. Files dropped to desks. Computer typing ceased. Phone calls paused.

Someone said, "Excuse me, sir, sorry. I think one of our team just received 'the phone call.'"

"Bev?" Jill said over the phone.

A coworker gripped my arm. "Bev, Bev, are you all right? Who died? Do you want us to go get your husband?"

"Bev," Jill repeated. "Why don't I call you back when you can speak? You're not going to lose the baby, I promise. If you want him, he's yours. Just take a few minutes to process."

We hung up. Fifteen minutes later, Jill called back. Still crying, I could talk—kind of.

After Jill's phone call, I sprinted to where my husband worked. He was perched on top of a helicopter. "Get down here!"

"I'm busy!"

"This'll only take a minute."

"What is it? Can't it wait?"

"Just, get down here, please?"

"Bev, I'm right in the middle of . . ."

Ugh. Men.

"I got *the call.* The adoption agency has a baby for us!"

His head perked up as did every other airman's. He shimmied to the ground and wrapped me in a huge, greasy hug.

I giggled and cried and sounded like I was choking. "We're having a baby!" The joy was so fierce in that moment, it didn't matter that the baby wasn't growing inside my belly. "We're having a baby!"

Since it was Friday, nothing more could be done until Monday. Over the weekend, time tortured me and crawled like a sloth overdosed on Valium.

More than once I swore at the clocks, "You must have stopped!" I raged with time itself. "What's taking you so long?"

Monday arrived. The agency opened at 9:00 a.m. I called at 8:44 . . . and 8:47 . . . and 8:53. At 8:58 someone picked up. "You've reached the adop—"

"Can I speak with Jill, please?"

"She's just walking in. May I place you on hold?"

Noooooooo! I added "hold" to my colorful list of 4-letter words.

"Sure. That's fine."

As I waited, I questioned whether Friday's call truly happened. We were so close, but I imagined a multitude of snags to prevent me from having my baby. I imagined Jill saying, "I'm sorry. There's a problem. The mother decided to keep her son." In that 45-second, on-hold-eternity, I worked myself toward a panic attack.

"This is Jill."

Sweet, blessed Mother Mary. "Hi Jill, this is Bev, the woman you called on Friday to say we have a baby."

She laughed politely. "Whoa, whoa, Bev, slow down a little."

I inhaled and shoved a breath out. "I wanted to check on the status of my son."

"Oh, Bev. Now, don't worry . . . " Her words "don't worry" triggered more anxiety.

"There's a slight problem."

Tears popped from my eyes, and I wailed. Jill cut me off.

"Bev," Jill's tone turned stern, but caring. "Bev. The mother still wants to give you the baby. She does not want the biological father to gain custody. It was a one-night stand. He's already moved on to another woman. He's toying with the idea of pursuing custody."

A sharp inhale wrapped a thin cloak of protection around my heart.

"—he doesn't have a leg to stand on, if it should come to a custody battle. If he brings the matter to court, he must also answer to statutory rape."

My breathing slowed. *Okay. Okay, okay, okay.*

Jill continued, "But if the mother relinquishes her rights first . . . "

Like someone dumped ice water on my head, reality cleared my brain and I interrupted, "Then the baby would go to him by default."

"Exactly. Don't worry, he'll sign. However, we must wait for him to sign first."

The closer I edged toward the possibility of adopting my son, the more my mind toyed with the unpredictable edges of the real world. Over the next few weeks, I should have walked around with a doctor and a crash cart on call.

Throughout those agonizing weeks, my heart stopped so many times. Every time Jill called, my breathing stopped anticipating the worst news.

After six weeks of hopefuls and hurts and hoops, the day arrived for my husband and I to meet our son.

A few days prior, I remarked to my mom, "I hope he's not ugly."

"What a terrible thing to say!"

"Well, I never got to hope for a boy or a girl. I never got to hope for a certain eye color or a healthy baby with ten fingers and ten toes, so I'm just gonna hope that my baby's not ugly."

My husband and I arrived at the adoption agency, then lugged our doctor and crash cart from the trunk—just kidding. The first sight of my son was the most beautiful thing I'd ever seen.

My heart stopped over and over and over again—the moment they placed him in my husband's arms. The moment my husband shifted him into my embrace. The moment we snapped him into his car seat. The moment we started the car to bring him home.

My son.

Even after all these years, I'm amazed how often people see my husband and son together and exclaim, "Oh! He looks just like you!"

We all just grin and say, "Thanks."

Hope that is delayed makes you sad, but a wish that comes true fills you with joy. Proverbs 13:12. ERV

Reflection: What's On My Heart?

Your uterus won't cooperate with your wishes to provide a temporary home for the baby you yearn for. A hysterectomy or adoption is not the right choice for every woman. To inhale your future, what anxieties do you need to exhale from your life?

What's the hardest struggle or decision facing you today?

What did you relate to in Bev's story that applies to your situation?

Dear Struggling Momma,

Confused about your next steps? Letting go of my ability and dreams to become pregnant was the hardest and best decision I ever made. Past moments that caused bitterness, now called forth joy.

My nephew and his wife moved for work and lived just over an hour from my husband and me. When their first two pregnancies ended in miscarriage, I reached out and walked alongside her through the pain.

One day she said, "Bev, you'll never know how much it means to me that you were there for me."

The day she went into labor, I was there. The baby girl was born by Caesarean. The nurse passed the tiny, screaming newborn to my burly, roughneck nephew. "Hey there, little one," he whispered. His daughter immediately calmed at the sound of his voice.

I watched from the other side of the glass as this tough, intimidating man cooed at his daughter. My nephew held his daughter first, the way my husband had cuddled our adopted son. I watched the nurses weigh and measure my great niece and guide my nephew through his daughter's first bath. It's a good thing parked crash carts and nurses on standby stood nearby, because my heart felt like it might explode.

My brother and sister-in-law lived two time zones away. With my phone glued to my ear, I excitedly narrated the play-by-play. I stood in the hospital room and snapped photos the first time my nephew's wife folded her arms around her baby girl. She hugged her husband. Then she grinned at me and said, "We had a baby!"

She and I were the "we." "That was the newest baby I've ever seen."

"It's about as new as they get," she said. "I was out of it. In those first few minutes, you saw more of her than I did. You may have even held her first."

I walked through the journey of her losses with her, and she delighted in sharing her joy with me. The birth was mine as much as it could have been. I'll never feel a baby kicking inside me. I'll never experience the thrill of pregnancy. I'll never share the news of a gender reveal. Sometimes, those thoughts still wrench my heart. However, overall, I encounter my grief much less than I did in the past.

God filled my life with love beyond my imagining. I'm grateful for the blessings He's granted me. May you find peace and joy in your life, too.

With Love,

Bev

The Pacific Northwest

18 What If I Never Have a Child?

Diane recalled with a soft bitterness. "On Mother's Day at church all the kids gave me flowers and then said, "You're my mother."

Diane wanted to say, "Well, I don't mean to be rude, but no, I'm not. You know?"

The kids wished Diane could bear children of her own. She was an amazing youth leader and would've made a fantastic mom.

Many chapters of my life overlap with Diane's life. We both grew up in the same church. We both carry a passion for youth ministry. We both experienced miscarriages.

Sometimes I wondered: *If Diane can't have children, will I be unable to bear children too?* Nothing logical followed this line of reasoning, so I constantly cauterized my heart against that possibility.

But what then? How did Diane deal with childlessness? She gifted her mom-heart to the children around her. A bit wacky with a touch of child-like agelessness herself, she created ways to interact with kids on their level. She hosted pool parties and sleepovers for her nieces and nephews.

She invited kids from church to ride on the RE/MAX float each summer for the Fourth of July parade. I can't believe that I deemed dressing up as a clown a good idea.

As a child, I endured health complications. Waking up in my hospital bed, I once saw Diane sitting beside me.

In college, I studied youth ministry. Excited to pass on books, wisdom, and advice, she mentored me. When her dad passed, she made certain that I received his hand-written Sunday School notes dating back to the 1950's were filed chronologically.

On one birthday, she pampered me with my first manicure, pedicure, and facial. Even though I lived two thousand miles away she visited me on the West Coast. And, every time, I hear Matthew 6:19–34, in which Jesus talks about serving God, not money, and laying up treasures in heaven where it's safe from moths and burglars, I think of her. Why? She encouraged me to memorize that passage.

I am only one person. Over the years Diane paid for braces, donated hefty camp and mission trip scholarships, provided babysitting, employed people who needed extra cash, rented out a small home on her property for people seeking refuge. Anyone whose life Diane touched was far better.

Why am I telling you all of this? Both Diane and Sandie experienced three pregnancy losses. Neither ever placed her infant in a car seat. I wish I could promise that everything will be okay for every mother who miscarries, but I can't. My heart is so heavy as I type these words: You and

I might not be able to bear and birth children, or more children.

So many people say, "Oh, don't worry. It'll happen."

Sometimes, I needed those words meant as encouragement. Most of the time, I cringed. "Oh, I'm sorry. I missed the fortune-teller credentials stuffed in your purse. How can you utter such an unfounded promise so flippantly?"

We know the truth: No human has any clue what our future holds. We may not get pregnant again. If we do, we may not carry the baby to full term. Throughout my young adult life I took for granted that children came easily. Didn't you?

According to the Centers for Disease Control and Prevention and the United States Department of Health and Human Services:

> *"Infertility is common. Out of 100 couples in the United States, about twelve to thirteen of them have trouble becoming pregnant. About ten in 100 (6.1 million) women in the United States, ages 15–44, have difficulty becoming pregnant or staying pregnant."*

If we don't receive a happy ending, what then?

Love. Love. Love. Love passionately. Love ferociously. Hold nothing back. I know this loss hurts. Hearing another woman's child gleefully cry, "Mommy!" and watching that child speed on a crash course toward that nice woman may grate like nails on a chalkboard. Mother's Day might feel like the suckiest holiday. No one has yet

invented magic glasses to shield piteous glances.

I can tell you from personal experience, if you're a Diane, that's not such a bad thing. I ran among the throngs of children who rushed to her on Mother's Day.

Mothers only received one carnation from each of their children. On more than a few Mother's Days, Diane received dozens of carnations from children eager to express their love and gratitude.

Because she possessed a mother's heart, Diane touched countless lives. She'll receive her reward in heaven for her love-in-action mom's heart. Plus her three heaven-borns will greet her when she arrives. She's Mom. We are moms.

Monica, mother of nine, never wanted children of her own. She always possessed a strong desire to adopt children existing in poor circumstances or children who lost or were abandoned by their biological parents.

God gifts us with a mother's capacity to love. In the midst of grief, your heart may feel leaky and leaden. Don't give up, please don't give up on loving. You're a parent who lost a child. Or you're infertile. Yet, you yearn to share your overflowing heart with a child. That's fantastic! Together, you and a neglected child could complete one another.

Others assured me that beyond the acute pain, God will mend our hearts. He desires abundance for us. Your love—a gift you can give to others—can never be extinguished.

Am I Enough?

A post-miscarriage daydream challenged my assumptions and expectations about motherhood. Jesus and I faced one another on opposite ends of a pale blue rowboat. Bright sky. No wind. Waves glopped against the wooden walls rocking the boat. The moment felt perfect until movement on a wide beach on the shore caught my eye. Mothers and children kicked up white sand as they played together. Their laughter carried across the water.

Jesus followed my gaze to the shore. "Sam, would you be okay if I were your only family? Just you and me, forever?"

"I guess . . . " The eyes of Truth saw straight through to my heart. I changed my answer. "No. No, Lord, I wouldn't be."

Jesus placed Clint in my boat. "Would he be enough," Jesus asked.

I shook my head "No." Before my miscarriage, I'd have answered, "Yes." My mom-heart overflowed with more love than Clint could ever handle.

In real life, sometimes I assault Clint with affection and he mutters, "So *much* with the kisses, so *much* with the kisses."

A downpour of teens drenched Clint, Jesus, and myself. Teenagers, who remained completely dry, clambered into the boat. I'm not sure where they came from.

Nick tripped into the boat, landing face first in front of Jesus. Levi, agile, leapt in behind him. Casi sat beside me. Other teens from the youth group piled in.

When the boat reached max capacity, more teens continued coming, scrambling atop each other's laps and falling onto the floor. Some hung off the side of the boat, while others sat half-in and half out.

Every teen I ministered to was present. They giggled and messed with one another. Their

Give your worries
to the Lord, and

he will care for you.

He will never let

those who are good

be defeated.

Psalm 55:22.

ERV

contagious laughter filled me with so much joy.

During the welcomed chaos, I spotted Jesus' knowing grin. As if he detected my loneliness, He rubbed his hands together and said, "Challenge accepted."

The commotion caused by teenagers broke our gaze. The entire boat erupted in laughter.

Love and laughter are imperative for survival. Hear this next sentence with tenderness: We cannot die inside just because our children died inside us.

Who has God placed in your boat? This world needs your love. This world needs you. You're valuable. You're counted. You're important.

If you ceased to exist, there would be an entire shipload of people who would miss out on quality life experiences. Grieve, by all means. For a short time, keep to yourself. Consume all the fast food you need to eat, but then recover. Don't wallow in pity—that's selfish.

Medical studies conducted by Dr. Seuss, author of *How the Grinch Stole Christmas,* proved serving others increases heart-growth. As Dr. Seuss wrote, "The Grinch's heart grew three sizes that day."

Brilliant.

From one miscarriage mother to another, get that big butt up and off your couch. Serve others. Expand your universe and your heart. To heal your soul, pursue serving others.

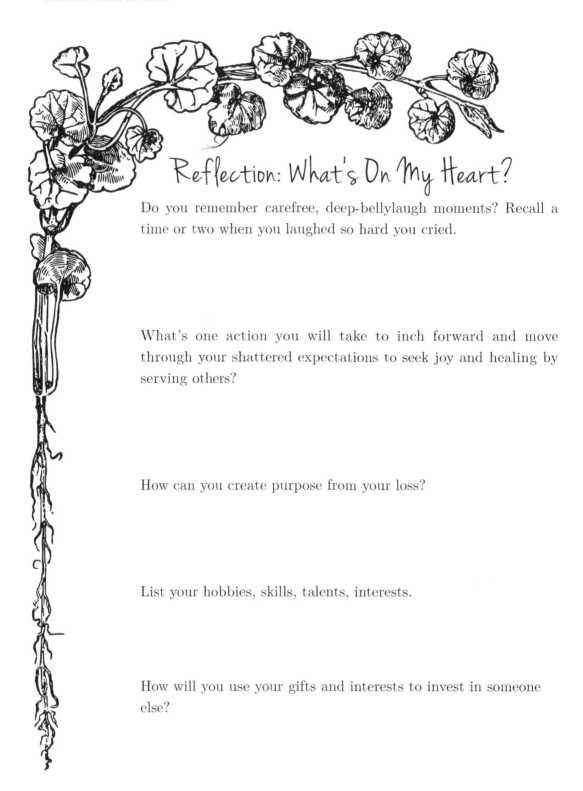

Reflection: What's On My Heart?

Do you remember carefree, deep-bellylaugh moments? Recall a time or two when you laughed so hard you cried.

What's one action you will take to inch forward and move through your shattered expectations to seek joy and healing by serving others?

How can you create purpose from your loss?

List your hobbies, skills, talents, interests.

How will you use your gifts and interests to invest in someone else?

In the Words of Others

Hey Darlin',

It's amazing, isn't it—how big the ache is for a child who brushed up against our lives so briefly? I've never held a baby who came from my own body. I used to cry because I'd never be a mom.

Sometimes I still choke up and think, "I'll never be a grandma."

But this big 'ol world needs women like you and me: Generous mamas with gigantic hearts, who have the time and money to give without holdin' back.

There are children everywhere. You just gotta find one or two or a whole classroom of 'em. It's an Easter egg hunt. You just gotta find 'em.

I found my kids when I started teaching Sunday school. The easiest, 'instant' births ever—35 church lovin' little heifers.

The boys look up at me with wacky grins and say, "We're boys, not heifers!"

I grin right back and say, "Your still my little heifers."

No matter what, they've got me, and I've got them.

Honey, you have a place in this world, too. And God is gonna use that tender, mushy heart of yours to bless the socks offa kiddos who are starved for love. God's got somethin' real special for ya, comin' right around the corner. You'll see. Hang in there, girl.

Love, Sandie

Oklahoma

19 Men, Miscarriage, and Mourning

"Clint, I miss our baby."

"I know," he whispered. He wrapped me in a bear-like embrace and kissed my bed-head hair. "I miss him, too."

Men don't share the same feelings or memories as women. Their bodies didn't change. Their hormones didn't infuse them with a super-charge of crazy. They didn't worry how the extra-large vanilla milkshake might affect their child.

Even so, the baby belonged to them, too. The second we knew, Clint called his parents and friends. "Dad! I'm going to be a dad!"

People warned us not to tell too many people too soon. We didn't understand why they cautioned us. Miscarriage never crossed our minds as a possibility.

Neither Clint nor myself dreamed the statistic for miscarried pregnancies was so high. People rarely speak of "failed" pregnancies. So, in our minds, we were pregnant and nine months later a baby would join our family.

Neither Clint nor myself fathomed an alternate reality.

TRIGGER ALERT: *If you prefer to skip the following graphic scene regarding the blood loss of miscarriage turn to page 207.*

"Clint! Clint!" He heard me calling from the bathroom. Shock belayed any inflection as I beckoned him. He still didn't know anything happened. We suspected, but until I called for him, hope and disbelief trumped a loss neither of us could fathom.

For me, the scene changed gradually from soothing, relaxing bubble bath to Stephen King murder scene. The tissue I passed transformed the bath water to a dark red. The water's color didn't register. My tunnel vision zoomed in on the baby I held.

Clint drew back the shower curtain and the entire reality shocked him. While nothing was funny about what we experienced, any humor in this situation pointed out the vast differences in perspectives between my husband and myself.

"Do you see the baby?"

With child-like innocence, I raised my open palm toward his eyes. I needed to know I wasn't crazy. *This is the baby, right?* My thick, hazy thoughts rendered me incapable of saying or doing anything to soften the blow to Clint. My shock prevented me from understanding that my actions were, well, a bit crazy.

His fist clenched the shower curtain. "Yeah, I see the baby."

He saw our dead baby and his wife, naked and vulnerable, bathed in a pool of blood, her blood.

"Why d-don't you shower so I can take you to the ER?"

His brain switched to autopilot. *Baby is gone. Protect wife at all costs.*

His wife never grasped his mindset at the right time. Going to the ER made complete sense to Clint.

When I could veg out in front of the TV, showering, drying, dressing, and biding time in a poorly lit ER made no sense to me. His suggestion sounded miserable, actually.

Besides, our baby was gone. Doctors couldn't bring Baby Evans back to life or slip the baby back into the womb. Why waste money on an unnecessary ER bill?

"Why would we go to the ER?" I finally noticed the red water. Right, so draining the tub is not the worst idea in the world. Neither is rinsing off. "I'm going to shower, okay Clint?"

"I'll be here if you need me."

By "here," I didn't realize he meant waiting in the bathroom, or I might have edited some of my outbursts. *I* knew physically, at least, I was fine. *Clint* feared I lost too much blood. Therein laid our point of disconnect.

I didn't anticipate the amount of tissue my body generated throughout the pregnancy. Clumps of tissue dropped to the floor. As the tub drained, what little emotional energy I still possessed drained away. Clint listened as I wept these words, "More blood, more blood."

Fearing I'd already lost too much blood, my husband plead, "Can I please take you to the ER?"

His question alerted me to his presence and startled me.

I cringed with embarrassment, recalling my outbursts to God. Clint heard everything. *He must think I'm insane.* The jolt of adrenaline I received upon hearing Clint's voice, snapped me out of the numbness of the grief vortex.

Awake now, I replayed our conversation and I saw what Clint witnessed.

"No. I'm fine. Clint, my body is cleaning itself out."

The image he absorbed of me in the bathtub finally penetrated my brain. I reassured him, "The bathwater diluted the blood. I haven't lost as much blood as you thought. This blood is extra blood, the baby's blood, not mine. I'm okay. I'm okay."

As I showered, I fell to pieces. *I'm not pregnant anymore.*

Clint sat on the toilet lid, powerless to fix what broke inside of me. For Clint, helplessness overshadowed the loss.

Later Clint told me, "I felt powerless and numb. I couldn't do anything to ease the hurt or erase our loss."

His child, his offspring died inside of me. To make matters worse, the death of the child tortured his lover. The most he could do was sit near the shower and observe the grief unfold.

His mind swarmed. *Was I not gentle enough with Sam? Did Sam carry something I should have insisted on lifting?* Clint desperately searched for a way to shoulder the blame, to share ownership of my pain.

One morning, all this became clear when he said, "If our next pregnancy ends in a miscarriage, then I'm going to get checked out by the doctor."

More than anything, his telltale statement revealed how desperately he wished to carry the burden.

"This isn't your fault."

He couldn't hear me. His ineptitude made him feel nauseous.

The morning after the miscarriage, Clint drove me to the doctor's office. After I changed into my clothes, I couldn't find him.

Eventually, I wandered outside. I didn't recognize him at first. Clint exudes strength and power—fearlessness. After a double-take, I realized the crumpled man on the bench was my husband. His crossed arms rested on his knees. His shoulders lay flush with his thighs, his head nearly between his legs. He sensed my presence and slow-motioned his upper torso to look up at me. Tears smeared across his face.

I eased down beside him, afraid to intrude on the reverence of the moment. "What was the breaking point," I asked quietly.

"That guy in the lab. That's when everything hit me—life's hard."

While the technician prepped me for a blood draw to measure my hCG levels, I asked him about the chalk sketch of an angel taped to the wall of his lab.

He tightened the elastic tourniquet at my upper arm. "My daughter, Sam, died in a motor-cycle accident. A friend of hers drew that picture to remind me of my angel. She was 19."

Outside with Clint, I rested my hand on his thigh. He clutched my hand. "I just needed some air."

"I've seen the white cross with her name on it,
Clint, at that intersection."

"Me too." He sighed. "And the one beside hers.
Wait. Is that where you talked to the girl?"

"Yeah."

Clint and I eased into silence.

Earlier that summer, I spotted a girl laying
flowers at Sam's cross. I felt compelled to stop my
car.

The sun shone. The wind whipped through my
tousled hair. I'd just been horseback riding, so
a layer of grime covered my everything. I didn't
smell amazing. Nonetheless, I parked on the
shoulder and crossed the two-lane highway.

As I approached, the girl watched me warily.

"Are you all right?" Dumb question. "Were you
friends with Sam?"

The girl nodded and wiped her nose on her
sleeve.

When I spoke Sam's name out loud, realization
dawned. *God, you placed me here. Give me
the right words.*

Humbled, I realized that no one else could
minister to this girl the way I could.

"My name is Sam . . . "

"Oh my God!"

"And I wanted to tell you that everything is
going to be all right. Sam is happy now, so you
should be too."

Tears burst from her eyes. "Can I . . . would
you think I'm weird if I asked you for a hug?"

"Not at all. I think that's why I'm here."

I hugged a stranger. Standing beside her friend Samantha's cross, she received a hug from Sam and a whispered assurance, "Everything is going to be all right."

Clint looked at me with watery, red-rimmed eyes. "We aren't alone, Sam," His words emerged scratchy. "Spouse, parent, child, friend . . . everyone loses someone. No one escapes life with a clean jersey."

Clint, my knight in shining armor, would do anything to make me happy or save me from pain. He wilted on the bench, as he realized some tragedies cannot be mended. No one escapes unscathed.

Several nights later, Clint ate at a restaurant with two guy friends. When he returned home, I asked him, "How did your conversation go?"

"We didn't talk about the miscarriage."

That makes no sense.

"What do you mean?" I blabbed to my friends, who graciously listened to details I'm certain they preferred never hearing. *How could Clint meet with his friends for a miscarriage pick-me-up without talking about the miscarriage?* "I'm confused."

"Well, they said they were sorry. What else could they say? There was nothing to say. Hanging out with them felt nice. We talked about other things."

Oh, ok. That answer made a bit more sense. I shook my head back and forth. *He's not coping the right way! Clint should talk through the*

loss for the sake of his emotional well-being.

Clint dove head first into the whirlwind of full-time school, completing the semester with a 4.0 GPA. *Okay, this is his coping mechanism. Could be worse.*

Even though a handful of times I feared he'd relapse back into alcohol—no one would've blamed him—he never reached for a bottle. *Maybe he's coping better than I realize.*

Why on earth I wanted more evidence, I'll never know. I continued to pester my poor husband about his emotions. Each time I mentioned the word "feelings," Clint scowled. I knew he held more thoughts prisoner in that thick 7-7/8-inch skull of his, but he never wanted to talk about it.

We women are so funny. We pick a little, or talk a little, or talk a lot to cope, gossip, process, grieve, celebrate.

Men . . .

No wonder I frustrated Clint so immensely. He knew how he felt. Why should he have to explain?

My pick-a-littles evoked maddening shrugs and grunts. My blood simmers remembering how I felt on the verge of pounding my fists on the floor in protest. *Answer me!*

I once asked a male friend, "So . . . when guys say they're thinking about nothing . . . "

"We're literally thinking about nothing."

If Clint wouldn't answer me, then I would do the next best thing—talk about him behind his back.

"Talk a lot. Pick a little."

In my defense, there was no premeditated assault. The opportunity presented itself when

Dia and I visited with one another. Her husband Dana ate at the restaurant with Clint after the miscarriage.

I asked Dana, "Did Clint ever say anything to you about the miscarriage?"

"Not a whole lot."

At least I'm not the only one. I studied Dana. As the husband of a wife who'd undergone multiple miscarriages, he seemed perfectly fine with "not a whole lot." Dana knew how Clint felt and filled in the blanks with his own feelings.

"He's just really angry," Dia explained that her miscarriages angered Dana.

Now, "he's just really angry," that's a full sentence there folks. Though piddly, Dana's answer was far more substantial than any words Clint offered. Progress had been had. I pushed my luck anyway—I wouldn't be me if I didn't.

Knowing Dana's answer, I lead the witness and asked, "Dana, did you feel angry, too?"

"Of course!"

"Why?"

"We had lost a child and there was nothing I could do to stop it."

Huh. That was the same impression I got from Clint—powerlessness. Maybe my husband wasn't holding as much back as I thought. Men don't lend descriptions of their feelings that fill the length of a book—oh look, like the one I'm writing. Their responses tend to be slightly shorter—like a word.

Can't write a book with one word. But Clint wasn't trying to write a book. He was only trying to please his wife. He sifted through his muddled brain glancing over frightening thoughts he knew better than to share with me. Clint protected me

Show mercy to others.

Be kind, humble, gentle, and patient.

Colossians 3:12b.
ERV

from the pain in his own psyche, and fell upon his white knight sword—with a safe word—powerlessness.

Even if he didn't give me the exact answer I desired, maybe I should be proud of him for a four-syllable word. I never doubted my best interest was at the core of my husband's heart. If he could, he'd take on my pain in half a heartbeat. I'd never stand a fighting chance of resistance.

Please be patient with your significant other, ladies. If he's not dealing with the loss like you think he should, don't worry. He hurts, too. He'll come around. Maybe for now, that's all you need to know—all he wants you to know—all he knows how to say.

"I love you. I'm hurting, too. I'll come around."

If he's anything like Clint, then months from now you'll hear one illuminating statement like a flash-paper fire—not a window to his soul. Really, more like a chopping block.

During a Sunday church service the pastor's sermon triggered Clint's chopping block attempt to communicate. At the time, I suspected Clint blurted out his feelings when my attention was one hundred percent focused elsewhere to make the sharing as painless as possible.

"I'm a wounded dog." He paused for a second, extremely impressed by the brilliant accuracy of his analogy. His eyes glimmered.

I glanced at him. "Huh?"

Clint's thought process was just as erratic as my pregnancy mood swings. He covered three different topics in the same paragraph. He used so many pronouns along the way, that when I stopped to clarify what Clint was talking about, my interpretation was almost always incorrect.

"That's exactly what I am," he agreed, still proud of himself, not exactly talking to me.

"Huh?" My eyes were dull as I waited for the explanation that would also answer the question, "What the heck are you talking about?"

"I'm a wounded dog. You know, a wounded dog gets hurt and needs help, but someone gets too close and . . . " His sentence ran out of steam.

"And the dog will bite him . . . huh?" I finished. Huh, as in, "oh, that makes good sense."

"Aren't I good with analogies? Chopping block down, Clint smiled. "I'm awesome at analogies. I like this pastor. I like the way he preaches . . ."

I smiled my pursed lip-dimpled smile while shaking my head, then I tuned back into Pastor Warren Stroup's sermon about the Prodigal Son. I glanced at Clint through my peripheral.

Wrinkled forehead, downward pointing eyebrows, and tight lipped, Clint studied Warren ad he spoke. "Huh. I didn't know that. Servants weren't allowed to wear sandals, which signified freedom. Did you know that, Sam?"

"No, I didn't." I whispered.

"Well, that makes sense, though. It's hard to run away without shoes on," Clint commented.

I laughed through my nose. Clint would be just fine.

Reflection: What's On My Heart?

Did your husband or boyfriend respond in the way you thought he should? Jot down memorable conversations with him, whether good, bad, or ugly.

In the Words of Others

Dear Moms and Dads,

It's Mother's Day 2013. After 4 weeks of bed rest and another stay in the hospital, my wife is set to head home tomorrow. She's fighting to keep our twin boys inside her. All of a sudden, she goes into labor.

Five hours later after nurses and doctors whiz in and out of our hospital room, she heads for emergency C-section. When our boys enter this world at 25 weeks and six days both weighing only two pounds, we're all scared to death. Doctors rush Adam and Ryan to the NICU.

"Six weeks," doctors encourage, "until we're 'out of the woods.'"

After six weeks, the doctors will try to remove the boys' incubators. The next six weeks, our entire world is reduced to machines beeping, blaring, alarming, fear-based adrenaline rushes, and doctor updates. We're too shocked to truly comprehend everything.

Week six arrives. We make our nightly visit and find Adam running a fever. Throughout the night the doctor runs tests.

Adam has NEC, which is basically intestinal inflammation. It's very serious. My wife and I stay with Adam overnight as he worsens. Within 24 hours, our sweet Adam has passed.

Ryan remains in the NICU. We count by days, weeks, then months. Every day we fight to find a reason of "why" Adam was taken from us. Every day Ryan's uphill battle terrifies us. My wife blames herself for the boys being born early.

As I struggle with my own pain, I struggle to be the rock she needs. Three months after Adam leaves for heaven, Ryan leaves the NICU to come home with Mom and Dad. We'd purchased items in two's, so his homecoming is bittersweet. We feel Adam's absence, but loving Ryan begins to mend our brokenness.

Now, seven-year-old Ryan and his little sister run circles in our backyard. Adam's portrait and name are displayed on our wall with the rest of our family. We speak of him often. My wife and I communicate well, which helped us through our difficult time.

The loss of Adam still hurts, but God has a plan. During those months in the hospital, I could not believe God had a plan.

Now I look back and wonder if Adam was sicker than we knew. Or maybe, in order to survive, Ryan needed a guardian angel to guide him through his fight.

Maybe your angel is guiding you, too.

You are not alone,

John

Woodridge, Illinois

20 Self-Care

Clint was far too proud of himself when an item was where he expected to find it. He said, "Ah ha! I Clint-proofed!"

Magna cum laude, my man. We're all simply confounded by his GPA. Nevertheless, I stole his phrase.

When I told him I plagiarized his words, he said, "Why not? You steal everything else of mine . . . stop wearing my deodorant."

I wasn't myself after my miscarriage. I knew I required more accountability than usual, so I set some self-care answerability in place to "Sam-proof, myself."

"Make sure I . . . "

"I need help with . . . "

Barb kept me in check with a daily workout routine, which helped me for multiple reasons. First, the familiarity of a routine fostered reassurance. Second, exercise required very little mental energy. Third, the endorphin kick—seriously—the boost helped. Exercise also helped get my body back in good physical shape.

With the miscarriage, I lost two pounds, but after one week of depression, I added eight pounds. I took off five pounds in one week when I cut out fast food, goodies in the cookie-cupcake family, and exercised several times. Exercise also rebuilt my self-esteem and self-confidence.

Endorphins, a natural warrior against the battle with depression, kick in after a cardio workout, not to mention other advantages: We can take our anger out on each stride, burn off those Burger King fries, and release pent up stress. When I work out, my mind unreels by sorting, processing, and unwinding.

The morning Barb and I ran two miles in the rain, the whole time I thought to myself: *Bring it on, world. I can take it. You're not going to keep me down.* This thought also immediately clicked the song *Chumbawumba Tubthumping* on a repeat track in my head.

Give your mind some freedom. You need time to come to terms with your new normal. Get your cardio on. Go for a walk, or a run, or a swim.

While your body is still recovering:

- **Go to bed earlier.** Exhaustion is normal after a miscarriage.

- **Eat a vegetable.** For the sake of our loved ones, we need to stay healthy. The healthier we eat and the more we work out, the better we feel.

- **Create a to-do list.** Many people around you want to help. They simply aren't sure how. So what do you need? Wouldn't help fixing your kids' lunches, or escorting them to the bathroom feel great? Do you simply want someone to sit with you? Any time someone offers help, refer to your list.

- Oh, look! A To-Do list! How did that get there?

  - Schedule a Mani/Pedi

- Complete 15 minutes of cardio
- Clean the kitchen
- Clean bathrooms
- Pick the kids up from school.

- **Ask friends and family for help.** When you tell people you've miscarried, most of them will likely say, "Oh, I'm so sorry! Let me know if there's anything I can do." Don't be afraid to say, "Well, actually. I need to clean my kitchen. Could you come keep me company while I clean?" Your friend will end up cleaning with you, and you may get even more out of the deal.

"Can I grab a coffee for you on the way over?" You respond, "Absolutely."

Grief of this magnitude doesn't come around every day. One day you'll pay it forward. When you hear about someone's miscarriage, you'll be on their doorstep with coffee and furniture polish in hand.

For now, accept the help you may not think you need. Be kind to yourself. Give yourself the gift of time to mourn, to relax, to recover, to heal. Lean on your support system. Eat healthy and get enough sleep, exercise, and time alone. Focus on your recovery.

Some moms find it hard to express what they need done. Below are some practice questions.

- "Can you watch my kids for a few hours?"
- "Could you help pack my kids' lunches?"
- "Will you go out to dinner with me?"
- "Can we watch a movie?"

Come to me all of you who are tired from the heavy burden you have been forced to carry. I will give you rest. Learn from me. I am gentle and humble in spirit. And you will be able to get some rest. Yes, the teaching that I ask you to accept is easy. The load I give you to carry is light."

Matthew 11:28–30.

ERV

Reflection: What's On My Heart?

Find an Accountability Partner

The grief vortex allures and entices. Zoning out appeals to me. For people prone to depression, the fight is even harder. You know yourself better than anyone. Do your best to protect yourself from yourself. Find an accountability partner—someone who will ask you the following hard questions.

- Did you shower today?
- Did you leave the house?
- What did you do today to seek out peace or joy?
- When was the last time you worked out?
- When was the last time you opened your Bible?
- Do you need to get out of the house tonight?
- Do you feel guilty?
- Are you up for some company?
- When is the last time you ate a healthy meal?

In the Words of Others

Dear One,

Yes. This terrible thing happened.

Shock, anger, pain. "Why, oh God—why? Just—why?"

Words of 'wisdom' come from well-meaning friends and family.

"You have four other healthy children."

"You can try again."

"This was meant to be."

"It's better this way."

Or my favorite: "The Lord knows best."

I trust God knows best—that didn't stop the tears, the tearing sensation in my gut.

Your spouse or significant other and your children might expect you to comfort them. Wait a minute! This is your body with a gaping hole.

This is your loss. There was life and then, there wasn't. There just wasn't.

As an oncology nurse, I often tell female cancer patients this is the one time its all about you. Women—let's face it—are usually the nurturers and caregivers, the ones who take care of everybody else. But now, for once, you need to take care of you.

For instance, friends call, just wondering how you are: Say as much or as little as you like. You owe no one an explanation. Screen your calls, or don't talk at all—your choice.

You wish to not attend a family party, or a church event? So, don't. Just say, "No thank you, I cannot attend." Again, you owe no explanation.

You want to take a soothing bath in the middle of the day? Drink a cup of tea while reading a book in your own quiet place? Do it.

Breathe, just breathe.

You won't forget this loss, but will you know joy again? Will you one day want to attend social events? Will you laugh and be happy again? Yes, resoundingly, yes. But you must take care of yourself to be a nurturer or caregiver.

For now—do what you need to do to heal. Take time for yourself. Take time to grieve. Healing doesn't happen overnight. But it will happen. And until it does—it's okay to be in your own mind.

It's okay for you to have times of quiet and calm, to cry, or simply remember. The whole world will be out there when you're ready. In the meantime—just breathe.

"Worry does not empty tomorrow of its troubles. It empties today of its strength," Corrie ten Boom.

Or as David states in Psalms 30:5, NIRV: "Weeping can stay for the night. But joy comes in the morning."

You will know joy again!

Mary

Illinois

21 Live A Life of Purpose

Doctors and Webster may define miscarriage as "a spontaneous abortion." I define miscarriage as the "unexpected, severed connection between a mother and child."

I will not say, "Everything happens for a reason." When people utter those words to me, anger of volcanic proportions erupts within me.

The purpose of life is connection.

Connection.

Comedians, sitcoms, advertisements, and reality shows attempt to connect with their audiences. A game even exists called "Six Degrees to Kevin Bacon," suggesting that any actor can be connected to Kevin Bacon through mutual actors, within six degrees. Social media posts go viral because people connect with what they see and hear.

Connection matters.

God created humans for connection—with Him and between one another.

The Lord God said:

> *"It is not good for the man to be alone. I will make a helper suitable for him." Then the Lord God made a woman from the rib he had taken out of the man, and he brought her to the*

man. The man said, "This is now bone of my bone and flesh of my flesh; she shall be called 'woman,' for she was taken out of man," Genesis 2:18; 22–23, NIV.

People matter. Souls matter. The Bible overflows with inspiring depictions of connection. The most sacred connection occurred when God clothed Himself with human frailty:

"The Word became flesh and made His dwelling among us," John 1:14a, NIV.

Jesus rubbed shoulders with humanity. To heal people with severe, contagious skin disease, He touched them. He shared His precious, limited time with social outcasts—to connect, to love.

Miscarriage, a severed connection, tears a mother away from her child. I will argue that miscarriage severs more ties than just a woman's relationship with her child.

On the blackest night following my miscarriage, I could not have been any sadder. If a parent, sister, or husband had died that week, I don't think I'd have experienced pain. While that statement sounds heartless and is heartless, I was heartless. Heart splintered. Heart broken. Heart empty.

Was it possible to be any more shattered than I already was? When love within us crumbles, the severance temporarily stunts our ability to connect with others.

Through the lens of miscarriage and severed connection, I read Luke 8:40–56. Luke, an author and a physician, overlaid one story of a 12-year-old girl with a mature woman. By Jewish tradition, the 12-year-old girl was just beginning woman-hood. The mature woman had bled vaginally for the entire length of the girl's life.

After meditating on the passage, I speculated on what Jairus, the father of a dying tweenager, and the woman might have felt. Did they possibly wish they'd rather be dead? Finding pieces of myself in each story, the prose below is my take on both stories and only conjecture.

As a woman plucked figs from a tree, a white-throated kingfisher fluttered down, landing upon a boulder. "I wouldn't get too close. My presence will soil you," she said. A frown wrinkled the woman's otherwise smooth face. Feeling exposed, her gaze darted up and down the road. *Just a few more minutes.*

The kingfisher cocked its head.

"Are you hungry too?" The woman reached toward the tree, pinched a fig between her fingers, and knelt near the bird. "Here you are."

She spent her last silver coin on another doctor who offered no more answers than the previous physicians. But she'd paid for his time to tell her nothing. Now her shekels purchased food for his table instead of her own.

Lost in thought, she didn't hear the baritone voices until the men were upon her. The kingfisher darted away.

Stripped of all dignity, she stood, cringed, and shouted, "Unclean! Unclean!"

The two men heading toward the city gates

glared at her. They edged to the opposite side of the road.

She remembered them from her childhood. Friends with whom she ran and played.

Now these two grown men were married with families of their own. *They might've chosen me for a bride if . . . well . . . things were different.*

Once, she took for granted that she'd sit included in the inner circle of mothers surrounded by children—one nursing at the breast, while two more swirled around her skirts. How lovely for children from her womb to barge into conversations she shared with other women.

A dream dead—buried.

As the men moved within the walls of the city, where she was no longer welcome, pieces of the men's conversation drifted on the wind. "Jesus," "disciples," " . . . this afternoon."

Jesus is coming here? If he can't heal me, no one can. She hiked up her grungy skirts as if to run toward town. Her ripe smell assaulted her. She dropped her skirts. Her head hung low. *Even if Jesus is willing to speak with me, no one will let me get close enough.*

She trudged back to her makeshift house, hidden from the road. *Will I ever swell with a baby? Will I ever create a home?*

The woman curled into a heap on the dirt floor and sobbed. Across the room hung a beautiful, blue gown the woman had intended to wear to the Temple in celebration when her hemorrhaging ceased. Twelve years later, the dress still hung in the same place. *I should just shred the fabric and use the scraps as menstrual rags.*

She leapt to her feet and fisted the cloth.

Sighed.

Released her hands.

No one will recognize me in that dress.

As if for the first time, she stared at her garment. She darted outside and plucked springs of lavender growing wild around her hovel. Back inside, she rolled the blooms between her palms, crushing the delicate buds. She dropped the tiny, bluish-purple blossoms into a shallow basin of murky rainwater.

Brown-and-crusted rags dropped from between her legs and plopped on the ground. She kicked the filthy material aside, picked up a stained-but-clean strip of cloth, and cleansed her broken body.

She drew her stiff dress over her head. *This will have to do.*

⚜

Jairus' mind remained at home, rather than on the Temple maintenance. He loved his daughter more than his own life. Her prognosis slowly killed him inside. Some days, he wished she'd just die to conclude his grief. More than he imagined possible, his heart bled for her.

His wife accused him of being unfeeling. Roping a tourniquet around his hope was the only way Jairus survived. That numbness erected a wall between his wife and him, locking intimacy beyond their reach.

His daughter lay dying. The silent haunt of Jarius' worst fears stalked his heart—with one fell swoop, he'd lose his daughter and his marriage.

Co-workers' sideway glances and cold shoulders only made matters worse. Their thoughts were easy enough to read: What sin did Jairus and

his wife commit to bring such tragedy upon their household?

Maybe they were right. I should turn around and offer a lamb on the altar behind me, just in case I unknowingly offended God.

"Jairus! Jairus!" His friend hissed his name and scurried toward him.

Jairus suspended scrubbing the brazen laver where ceremonial washing took place. Dimwitted gossips, who patrolled the streets beyond the Temple, stood close by.

His friend scanned for eavesdroppers, then whispered, "Jesus, the healer. Jairus, Jesus is coming into town today."

"My daughter. . ."

His friend nodded. "Go!"

"Do you think He'll speak to me?"

"You're a leader in the synagogue, of course He will!" He yanked the rag from Jairus' hands. "Go! I'll cover for you."

Jairus hiked up his robe and sprinted away.

An excited crowd, who expected Jesus, swarmed around him. Jairus fell at Jesus' feet. A woman crouched behind Jesus and lightly touched the hem of his robe.

In the crush of the crowd, Jesus felt power leave him. He asked, "Who touched me?"

As Jesus was distracted, anxious thoughts filled Jarius' mind.

The woman seeking healing fell at Jesus' feet, then told Jesus she touched the hem of his robe, and her bleeding stopped.

As Jesus talked with her, "Daughter, your faith has healed you. Go in peace—"

A man interrupted, "Jairus, your daughter died. Don't bother Jesus."

Jesus turned to Jarius, "Don't be afraid; just believe, and she will be healed." Jesus left the crowd and walked to Jairus' home with his disciples trailing behind.

Before Jairus saw his wife, he heard her wailing. *So it's true, then. Our daughter is dead.* His wife's cry slashed through his heart.

The crowd, who gathered outside his home, saw Jairus approaching and parted. His wife curled in a fetal position on the ground, her sister wrapped around her. Sobs heaved her body up and down.

"Jesus," a man murmured. The name trickled from person to person in hushed wonder.

"Stop wailing," Jesus said. "She's not dead but asleep."

Gossips, looking for a story to spread, erupted in laughter.

Embarrassed, Jairus' wife rose to her feet, squeezed Jairus' hand and glared at Jesus. *Does He mean to mock us?*

"Trust," Jairus whispered, as if reading her thoughts.

The laughter beyond the door faded as they led Jesus to the room where their daughter lay. At the sight of her daughter's grayed lips and vacant face, Jairus' wife burst into a fresh onslaught of tears.

Jairus wept silently, tears dropping into the rich fabric of his wife's head covering.

Jesus glanced at Peter, James, and John as if to say, "Take notes. One day you'll tell this story."

Jesus gazed at the girl's parents. Peace radiated from his countenance. Fears died away. The sobs subsided. Without words, Jesus carried them into

a sacred place where death and life meet.

Jesus touched Jairus' daughter's lifeless body. His touch connected with her soul and raised her to life. Through this act of *agape*, the highest form of love, Jesus shared a secret with the girl's parents: Death is not the end.

><>< ><>

Journal Entry A.D. 31: Eight days ago, I felt Jesus brushing shoulders with me, unafraid to be labeled "unclean" in order to touch me, unabashedly balking at social etiquette to speak with me. I'm not just a face in a crowd. Jesus stopped to connect with me. I matter.

Today at the Temple, where I wore my blue dress, I bathed in the mikvah as prescribed after bleeding has stopped before presenting my sacrifice. I caught a glance of the man whose daughter died. Rumors are flying around the village that she was only asleep. I exchanged a knowing glance with the man at the Temple, and I knew the truth.

Jesus brought me back from the brink—and not only me. Jesus didn't swear my healing to secrecy like he did Jairus. Women in the village embraced me and welcomed me home. This afternoon, I moved in with my cousin and her brood. She said her neighbor looked my way.

Even if nothing comes of it, I am not alone. I'm renewed with hope. Today is a new day.

✈

I always pictured the woman as old—far beyond menopause and childbearing years. Nowhere in Matthew 9:18–24, or Mark 5:25–34, or Luke's accounts, do the authors mention her age. Mark 5:26, NIV states:

> *"She had suffered a great deal under the care of many doctors and had spent all she had, yet instead of getting better she grew worse."*

Doesn't that sound like polyps, cysts, fibroids, or endometriosis, or other chronic bleeding conditions that lead to infertility?

Perhaps the woman was elderly. She might have once been married and then discarded. Maybe she miscarried and never stopped bleeding. She may also have been single and as young as 24, never arriving at the wedding bed to discover she was infertile. No man would want her.

I can only speculate about the details, but I related to her much more easily once I considered she might not be 107 years old. Typically, women cycle twelve times a year. This woman bled for twelve years straight.

Shame. Guilt. Questions. Anger. Dead dreams. We're the bleeding woman. Physically bloodletting, emotionally bleeding out. We're mothers, who through bloody means, lost connection with our child.

Luke draws parallels between the woman and Jairus. Desperate and suffering, lifeblood drained from both the woman and Jairus' daughter. With faith, the woman and Jairus turned to Jesus, their last resort, for healing. The woman, a penniless, powerless social outcast sought healing. And Jesus, whose power healed on behalf of the family-less woman, calls her daughter.

The man, who begged on behalf of his daughter, lived in an affluent position of elite power, yet powerless to prevent the death of his daughter. Both humbled themselves and took a risk to connect with Jesus and to trust Him.

Desperation, suffering, and tragedy is not biased. Regardless of age, social rank, or gender, anguish and death confronts both the powerful and the powerless. As we see in Luke 8, Jesus' compassion is not partial, either.

You and I grew up in different places with different families in differing social standings. We attended different schools and differ on many beliefs. We possess different amounts of money in our bank accounts and enjoy different hobbies.

Despite our differences, we're all the bleeding woman. We're also parents grieving the death of a child.

On this one issue—losing a child—we're bonded, connected, sisters. In this sacred place that connects us, Jesus shares a secret: Death is not the end, but a resurrection to a new life.

He was present at each child's deathbed. He connected with and touched our babies and raised them to eternal life.

No matter who you are, what you've done, what you've left undone, or how much stock you place in this whole Jesus thing, you matter to God. You are loved. He invites us all into a reverent place of connection with Him.

If the purpose of life is connection, and miscarriage severed that connection, how do we reconnect?

One day at a time. Healing starts incrementally, then gains momentum. Means of connection present themselves.

Love Letters to Miscarriage Moms is my version of my child's purpose. This book provides my opportunity to connect with you, to remind you that you are loved. Your gifts, talents, and purpose differ from mine.

As you walk forward, step by step, I believe you'll find a way to honor the life of your child by connecting with yourself. Connecting with your spouse. Connecting with other miscarriage moms. Connecting with Jesus.

Release any preconceived notions about any grief duties you feel required to perform, or any pressures others place on you. The sun shines without our help. Settle for imperfection. We can't freeze in place altogether. However, we can slow down to reflect upon loss, life, and purpose.

Life is a gift, a precious, precious gift. Each life also has a purpose, which may be hard for you to understand right now.

Our babies all had a purpose on this earth as well. Look at mine—he or she gave me sympathy for miscarriage, which I never understood. I wrote a book, for goodness' sake.

Your baby had a purpose too. Maybe your baby or babies lived to realign your crosshairs. Maybe you're supposed to share your story with someone else struggling to make sense of her loss. Think of

After you have suffered a little while, our God, who is full of kindness through Christ, will personally come and pick you up, and set you firmly in place, and make you stronger than ever.

1 Peter 5:10, TLB

all the women you've heard about who miscarried before you did. What was your response?

You've acquired a deeper love. Did your baby teach you how to love better?

One day, Misty said, "You're truly a mom, you possess a mother's heart. You know what sacrifice is—and unconditional love."

We thought about every food morsel entering our mouths in a whole new way. We wondered how various activities affected our child. We cared for our children when they couldn't give us anything in return. Their presence inside of us was enough.

Your child changed your life. You're the only one who will know your child's purpose fulfilled. The biggest way to honor your child is to continue living. Cherish life.

Jesus, our hope fulfilled, our hope rewritten, said,

"I am the light of the world," John 9:5, NIV.

Jesus lived a life of purpose. His purpose? To give His life to exchange our darkness with His light. It wasn't enough for God to look in on our pain from heaven. He decided the only way to truly love us was to come to earth and live among us.

Jesus, who reflects His Father God, lived as a human with a limited-life warranty. The last instruction He doled out to the disciples before ascending to His throne as our King was, "Go! Get off your duff and tell people about me," my loose paraphrase of Matthew 28:18–20.

For inasmuch as Jesus promised to be our hope and light in our darkness, He also called us to offer hope and light to others.

You're here to be light, bringing out the God-colors in the world. God is not a secret to be kept. We're going public with this, as public as a city on a hill. If I make you light-bearers, you don't think I'm going to hide you under a bucket, do you? I'm putting you on a light stand. Now that I've put you there on a hilltop, on a light stand—shine! Keep open house; be generous with your lives. By opening up to others, you'll prompt people to open up with God, this generous Father in heaven," Matthew 5:14–16, MSG.

My first response to offer hope and light? I resisted and fought a good five-hour fight (4¾ hours of which I slept) only to learn that fighting God is useless. Even in the middle of my darkest grief, I sensed that God wanted me to write this love letter to you.

Now He tugs at your heart to be someone's love letter from God. God calls us to tangibly love others the way Jesus loved the woman with the issue of blood and the parent who lost all hope.

A phone call from friend, who lost a lifelong friend in Afghanistan, intruded upon my plans for the day. A quick reminder of those who listened to me throughout my grief shushed the part of me uninterested in a long conversation.

My friends and family acted as Christ to me. Now this opportunity interrupting my plans for the day presented my turn to give back and offer Christ's love, compassion, and comfort.

My job and yours is to notice the needs and the hurts of people around us. If you're not in a place to bend or stoop in kindness toward another, lend yourself grace.

God gave each of us gifts to share with others. Do you sing? Do you write? Can you draw more than a stick camel? Are you good with numbers? Do you knit? Are you good at puzzle-solving or repairing anything mechanical? Can you listen? Can you spare three dollars to buy a friend coffee or a homeless man a hamburger?

Are you working up courage to share your story—not just your miscarriage story—any story about how God worked in your life? Each mentioned and unmentioned talent supplies a way to connect with others and live a life of purpose.

As I closed out the few remaining pages of writing the first edition of this book, the end of December approached. According to the church calendar, the season of advent had begun.

Advent, the time of anticipation before celebrating Christ's birth, poses questions to reflect upon: Are you ready? Is it time yet?

Four candles at the front of the church represented the four weeks of advent. A banner under each candle listed words that encompassed the season of advent. Peace. Joy. Hope. Love.

These are good words, amen? These are very good words.

As I reflected on each word, the anticipation of the blessings God promised stayed close to my heart. God, is it time yet? I'm a young girl all over again, trapped in the backseat of my dad's minivan on a twenty-seven hour road trip to Florida from Chicago. Are we there yet? How about now?

At our first advent service after my miscarriage, our pastor asked me to read Luke 2:1–7, NIV:

> *"In those days Caesar Augustus issued a decree that a census should be taken of the entire Roman world. (This was the first census that took place while Quirinius was governor of Syria.) And everyone went to their own town to register. So Joseph also went up from the town of Nazareth in Galilee to Judea, to Bethlehem the town of David, because he belonged to the house and line of David. He went there to register with Mary, who was pledged to be married to him and was expecting a child. While they were there, the time came for the baby to be born, and she gave birth to her firstborn, a son. She wrapped him in cloths and placed him in a manger, because there was no guest room available for them."*

My voice echoed in the speakers. As I read the passage to the congregation, a word in the margin distracted me. Years before pregnancy ever entered my mind, I scribbled next to the Luke passage this word: "Hope." That word brought a smile to my face, because my heart harbored a secret.

Reflection: What's On My Heart?

How do the following verses speak to your heart? In the spaces below, jot down the connection you observe between Jesus and others. Then note the connection between you and God.

"The Word became flesh and made his dwelling among us. We have seen his glory, the glory of the one and only Son, who came from the Father, full of grace and truth." John 1:14, NIV.

"In your life together, think the way Christ Jesus thought. He was like God in every way, but he did not think that his being equal with God was something to use for his own benefit. Instead, he gave up everything, even his place with God. He accepted the role of a servant, appearing in human form. During his life as a man, he humbled himself by being fully obedient to God, even when that caused his death—death on a cross." Philippians 2:5–8, ERV.

"I am the Vine, you are the branches. When you're joined with me and I with you, the relation intimate and organic, the harvest is sure to be abundant. Separated, you

can't produce a thing. Anyone who separates from me is dead-wood, gathered up and thrown on the bonfire. But if you make yourselves at home with me and my words are at home in you, you can be sure that whatever you ask will be listened to and acted upon. This is how my Father shows who he is—when you produce grapes, when you mature as my disciples." John 15:5, MSG.

"When Jesus saw his mother there, and the disciple whom he loved standing nearby, he said to her, "Woman, here is your son." John 19:26, NIV.

"While Jesus was in one of the towns, a man came along who was covered with leprosy. When he saw Jesus, he fell with his face to the ground and begged him, "Lord, if you are willing, you can make me clean."

Jesus reached out his hand and touched the man. "I am willing," he said. "Be clean!" And immediately the leprosy left him." Luke 5:12–13, NIV.

"As Jesus and his disciples were leaving Jericho, a large crowd followed him. Two blind men were sitting by the roadside, and when they heard that Jesus was going by, they shouted, 'Lord, Son of David, have mercy on us!'

"The crowd rebuked them and told them to be quiet, but they shouted all the louder, 'Lord, Son of David, have mercy on us!'

"Jesus stopped and called them. 'What do you want me to do for you?' he asked.

"'Lord,' they answered, 'we want our sight.'

Jesus had compassion on them and touched their eyes. Immediately they received their sight and followed him." Matthew 20:29–34, NIV.

"While Jesus was still talking to the crowd, his mother and brothers stood outside, wanting to speak to him. Someone told him, 'Your mother and brothers are standing outside, wanting to speak to you.'

"He replied to him, 'Who is my mother, and who are my brothers?' Pointing to his disciples, he said, 'Here are my mother and my brothers.' For whoever does the will of my Father in heaven is my brother and sister and mother." Matthew 12:46–50, NIV.

"Now when Jesus returned, a crowd welcomed him, for they were all expecting him. Then a man named Jairus, a synagogue leader, came and fell at Jesus' feet, pleading with him to come to his house because his only daughter, a girl of about twelve, was dying.

As Jesus was on his way, the crowds almost crushed him. And a woman was there who had been subject to bleeding for twelve years, but no one could heal her. She came up behind him and touched the edge of his cloak, and immediately her bleeding stopped.

" 'Who touched me?' Jesus asked.

"When they all denied it, Peter said, 'Master, the people are crowding and pressing against you.'

But Jesus said, 'Someone touched me; I know that power has gone out from me.' Luke 8:40–46, NIV.

In the Words of Others

Dear Mama:

Welcome to the club that no woman wants to ever join. I'm so sorry you're here, but you'll find strength and support like nowhere else on the planet. The women who have come before you are strong and brave and beautiful and broken. Just like you.

At a time when nothing made sense in my world, I found my greatest comfort in serving those who were grieving. Solidarity in grief provides healing. We can lift each other up, especially when we're hurting, because we relate to each other in a way no one else can. We can meet the grieving where they are. Because we're there, too.

If you need to stay in your pj's for a couple days and eat ice cream from the tub while binge watching Netflix, that's cool, too. But when you're ready, I hope you'll find strength and purpose in acts of kindness to others.

Blessings!

Andrea,

Wisconsin

22 That's Not a Wrap

Did you guess my secret? I intended to begin this chapter with these words: "I'm pregnant."

Then I deleted that sentence. We lost another baby.

As I typed each chapter, I thought, *Wouldn't it be awesome to end the book with a pregnancy announcement?* Turned out, I *was* pregnant again a few days after the nurse's phone call telling me, "You're not pregnant."

I enjoyed the story of getting pregnant two weeks after my first miscarriage—Good idea, God! My blessing fulfilled. Like the bleeding woman, I felt redeemed.

However, the Author intended a different ending.

When I miscarried my second pregnancy, fears assailed my thoughts. *Maybe something's wrong with me. I won't chase away this demon until I successfully carry a child to full term. Be careful.*

I guarded my heart more throughout my second pregnancy. Clint, too. Finally, he acknowledged the guard he placed around his heart. My second pregnancy advanced farther than the first one.

The due date fell within days of my father's birthday. At first, the pregnancy felt healthier. I switched to maternity pants and stored all my non-maternity clothes that wouldn't fit for *a long time*. That thought brought me so much joy.

Four days from our first ultrasound, I imagined delivering the pictures of the sonogram to family members in Christmas cards.

I counted down the days to text Debi again saying, "Um . . . gonna be a little bigger for your wedding."

Clint and I arranged our summer plans around the birth of this child.

And then . . . I started spotting. Cramps kicked in. I 'prayed.' My words certainly weren't the traditional kneeling quietly beside the bed with palms pressed together and whispering sweet nothings to God.

Throughout the day, I shouted, "Please, Jesus! Please, Jesus! Please, Jesus! Please, Jesus! Please, Jesus!" Occasionally, I added the coherent thought, "You're the only one who can save this baby!"

I sang the lyrics to the song *Praise You In This Storm* recorded by Casting Crowns, I gasped mid-song at the words the Holy Spirit stirred inside me: *I'm about to encounter another storm.*

My brain short-circuited on Bible verses while my suffering flesh waged war with the theologically trained and Scripture-savvy Bible geek locked inside my heart. I reminded God about faith-filled individuals in well-known Bible stories, who refused to accept "No" for an answer.

Shoving aside the acceptance of another miscarriage, I mentioned to Jesus the officer in the Roman army, who wasn't a religious insider.

The centurion sent a faith-filled message to Jesus:

> *"Just say the word, and my servant will be healed. For I myself am a man under authority, with soldiers under me. I tell this one, 'Go,' and he goes . . . ,"* Matthew 8:8–9a, NIV.

Jesus, you helped a religious outsider, a pagan woman, who recognized Your identity, compassion, and power to heal her daughter. She knelt before You to beg for crumbs:

> *"Even the dogs eat the crumbs that fall from their master's table,"* Matthew 15:25, NIV.

I persisted and called Jesus' attention to His parable about the poor, powerless widow, who pled her last, and only hope to a cold-hearted, corrupt judge. Only after pestering the wicked judge, who didn't care about justice or the welfare of others, he helped her. (Luke 18:1–8)

I persevered and reminded Jesus of all the people He healed and all those He raised from the dead. I knew the miscarriage wasn't His fault, but I also knew He possessed the power to stop this miscarriage.

I promised to give Him all the credit for saving my child from the brink of death, as if offering Jesus a favor in return for saving my baby.

Bargaining.

Then I stomped my foot and yelled, "This was the blessing You promised me!"

Anger.

The only clear words I heard from Him that night were, "No, Sam, it wasn't."

At first, I didn't hear His words. I didn't want to hear them.

Denial.

What I did I do to cause You to turn Your face from me. Why aren't you answering my prayers?

Depression.

Another child born too soon.

Soon after that miscarriage, I made a silly decision. I attended a funeral. I thought I kept myself together pretty well . . . until jealousy, of all emotions, blindsided me.

She met my children before me.

The Holy Spirit reminded me, "Never your children to begin with."

I don't excel at the concept of surrendering or the word "no." Do you?

Not long after the funeral, the phone rang at the church. Because the office was closed on Fridays, I didn't usually pick up the phone. No one knew I was there. I intercepted a distress call from a frantic woman in our congregation, who needed immediate prayer for her daughter. I prayed with her, hung up the phone, and continued working.

Five minutes later, I received a text from her:

"Wow! God is good."

God favorably responded to her impossible situation—*in five minutes.*

The rest of the evening a dark, Eeyore storm cloud hovered over my head and heart. "*Why her, God? Why her? You answered her prayer in five minutes, but with me, You remain silent."* I noted the time on the clock—11:28 p.m.

Yet, God answered my prayer as much for me as He had for her: "Sam, I still hear you. I'm still listening. Your prayers are still getting through."

Real life isn't like the chick flicks I enjoy in which the heroine always gets what she wants after 122 minutes. When she lives out her happy ending, whatever struggles she endures prove worthwhile.

We all cycle through times of happiness, but the end credits never roll there. Time advances, propelling our lives forward, a never-ending story with future pages yet to be written. Our lives aren't choose-your-own-adventure books, where we backtrack and rewrite the outcome we prefer.

In my quieter moments, I reflected on Job and Hannah. In light of my miscarriages, some thoughts occurred to me regarding Job and Hannah's stories, details that carried a different meaning. Job lost all his adult children, his income, and all his wealth in one day, then endured an excruciating skin disease to boot.

In Job 1:7–12, Satan, who roamed the earth to steal, kill, and destroy, prowled like a lion stalking prey. The Prince of Darkness stands before the Lord who directs Satan's attention toward a man faithful to God, who refuses to do evil.

Satan challenges God, "Of course Job praises you. Of course he goes around singing, 'Wow, God is good.' If I destroy everything Job has, I promise he will curse You to Your face."

The Lord said to Satan, "All right, do whatever

you want with anything that he has, but don't kill Job."

After so many devastating losses and with boils covering his body, Job questioned God. In the end, he praised the Lord. The way Job handled his loss testified to everyone who knew his story of loss.

> *"Then Job answered the Lord: 'I know that you can do all things. No plan of yours can be ruined. You asked, 'Who is this that made my purpose unclear by saying things that are not true?' Surely I talked about things I did not understand. I spoke of things too wonderful for me to know,'"* Job 42:1–3, ICB.

1 Samuel 1:19 relates Hannah's story. Year after year, Hannah, who's infertile, accompanies her husband to Shiloh, the temporary home of the Ark of the Covenant and the Tabernacle. Shiloh, which means "place of rest," provided no rest for Hannah's yearning to bear a child.

Bitter to the soul, Hannah weeps from the depth of her grief as she petitions God to give her a child. She prays:

> *"Lord of heaven's armies, see how bad I feel. Remember me! Don't forget me. If you will give me a son, I will give him back to you all his life,"* 1 Samuel 1:10-11, ICB.

The Lord remembers her pleas, and in time Hannah gives birth to a son. Hannah says, *"His name is Samuel because I asked the Lord for him,"* 1 Samuel 1:20, NIV.

God answers her prayer in His perfect timing. God used Hannah's son Samuel to play a critical role in a pivotal part of history, in specific places at specific times.

Samuel, a prophet of the Lord, anointed Saul as Israel's first king. He also anointed David as king. In God's scope, Hannah's son was not born too soon or too late, but at the perfect moment to fulfill God's plan.

These stories triggered so many questions:

- Why me?
- What next?
- What happens now?
- Will I bear children?
- What blessing did God refer to and when do I cash in the chips on the blessings deal?
- If the timing wasn't right, why did He allow me to get pregnant twice?

Then God asked questions, too.

- Am I your God *only* when things go well?
- Do you trust Me *only* when life is good?
- Is your love for Me based on blessing?
- Do you know that I love you? That I have not forgotten you? That I never will abandon you?

The way we handle our losses testifies as well. Has your miscarriage affected your view of God's character? Did two miscarriages in three months shake my faith? Yes. Destroy my faith? No. God is still God. Those miscarriages didn't dethrone Him. I believe God knows what He's doing.

My relationship with God wasn't always peachy-keen, like when I said to God, "If you were tangible, I'd punch you."

I'm pretty sure this is not the way the Creator of the universe deserves to be talked to—but I'm certain my comment hurled at God, didn't throw Him off guard, either.

God maintains sole rights to my innermost thoughts. Despite this fact, He still sticks around: He still loves me, which is a miracle in itself.

My third miscarriage began on a Sunday morning during a church service. I felt the cramps . . . the moisture in my underwear. And I knew. I tossed my second daughter, Kelly, to a friend and sprinted to the bathroom. I yanked up my dress and ripped my underwear down and saw the blood. "No, no, no, no, no, no."

After that miscarriage, again I shared some choice words with God, "I learned this lesson already! I wrote a stinkin' book about it, for heaven's sake. It's good! You should read it!"

I once read on the back of a sugar packet: "Friends are people who know all about you but like you anyway." That's the best characteristic about God.

I'm a spoiled, selfish, sinful woman, and He still cares about what I say. When I pray, He takes my words into consideration. However, He doesn't let me act like a spoiled princess when I know better.

While throwing a spiritual hissy fit, I journaled an imaginary conversation with God.

As I vented, I also imagined God's response.

I intuited God declaring, "Enough is enough."

Me: I want *my* way.

God: Do you trust me?

Me: Yes, but . . .

God: Are you ready to be blessed?

Me: Yes, but only if it means having things MY way. I know how I want to be blessed. I have some great ideas . . . I could share them with You if You'd like.

God: *Delight yourself in the Lord and He will give you the desires of your heart,* Psalms 37:4, ESV.

Me: That's a trick verse. If I'm delighting myself in You, then Your desires will become my desires. You will give me what I want because what I want has become exactly what You want. But I still want what I want. I'm just not there yet.

God: *Humble yourself and the Lord will lift you up in due time.*(1 Peter 5:6)

Me: Give You *everything*? My dreams, too? My plans, my hopes, my wishes? Lord, I'm sorta attached to them. They're *mine.* I'll give You my time. I'll share my talents. I'll tithe. If You need me to, I'll even give up to 11% of my income after taxes.

God: I don't *need* anything from you. I want *you.*

Me: But Lord, what will you do with my dreams, my hopes? Will you still give me what I want? Or maybe, You gave me my desires, my wishes, dreams, and hopes. Maybe they were Yours all along.

God: There's only one way to find out.

Me: Wait, was that a yes or a no? I know you

think I'm stubborn, but sometimes I think you created me that way on purpose—just so we could have conversations like these. You're entertained. I can tell.

God: Do you trust me?

Me: Sigh.

God: Am I your God *only* when good things happen?

Me: No, I guess not.

God: Do you trust me? Are you ready to be blessed?

Me: Ugh! Sometimes I just want to box You, You know?

God: Bring it on.

Me: I feel like this world wants to have its way with me.

God: You're mine. You're fighting me, but I'm fighting for you.

Me: Sometimes I feel like giving up, letting the world win.

God: I'm jealous for you. They won't win. Are you ready to be blessed?

God's ways are higher than ours. While you and I only focus on one piece of the seven-billion-plus pieces of the jigsaw puzzle, His eyes absorb the entire panorama.

Despite His super-busy schedule, He'd still leave heaven in a flash—His throne, His deity, His authority, and trade all of His divine privileges for the bruises that accompany this life to connect with us, and tell us face-to-face, "You're not alone."

Wait! His Son already did!

Even if we don't get our way, we're never alone.

Clint spoke to the teens about following Christ the way Christ deserves to be followed. My endearing, spirit-filled, genius idiot said, "It's gonna be hard—but God is harder."

I liked the quote so much I typed those words and hung a poster in the youth room. Each time I ran in that room to make a phone call, that poster, plastered to the wall above the phone, stared back at me. Clint's quote reminded me that my God is tougher than any challenge I'll ever face.

Are you strong enough to trust Him? To worship Him, even if you never get your way? To see the goodness of God shining through your darkness?

Follow. Obey. Love. Go. No disclaimer statements: "Only when I feel like it."

Jesus didn't shout, "Yipppeeee!" or sing, or dance, or skip His way to the cross. Every step was difficult.

He even asked His Heavenly Father:

> *"Father, remove this cup from me. But please, not what I want. What do you want?"* Luke 22:42, MSG.

Jesus never dictated to His Father, He surrendered to His Father's will to restore our broken relationship with God.

We didn't deserve for Jesus to trade places with us. (Romans 3:23) Yet, He loved us so much that Jesus endured the cross anyway.

God gave His only Son for us and Jesus gave His life for us.

We can't ever tip the scales in our favor.

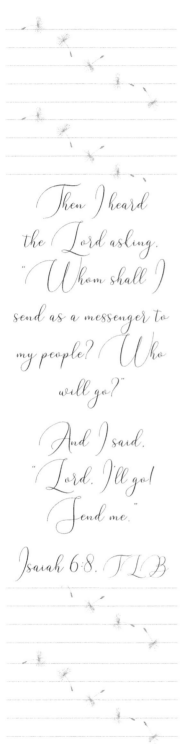

Then I heard the Lord asking, "Whom shall I send as a messenger to my people? Who will go?"

And I said, "Lord, I'll go! Send me."

Isaiah 6:8, TLB

Wouldn't you agree, that it's a good thing our God is not a god of 'You can only get to heaven if . . .' disclaimers?

God doesn't play that manipulative mind game. Neither should we.

"I'll only follow You if . . . "

Come now, don't you think God deserves more than stale leftovers?

Emotionally bankrupt, I appealed to Him for help. My reflection in the mirror was far from impressive. And yet, Jesus invited:

> *"Come to me all of you who are tired from the heavy burden you have been forced to carry. I will give you rest. Accept my teaching. Learn from me. I am gentle and humble in spirit. And you will be able to get some rest,"* Matthew 11:28–29, ERV.

After my three miscarriages, praising God was as easy as bench pressing a Buick. All I had to offer him was a broken heart and empty hopes.

Yet, God wants me just as I am. God doesn't need my money, acts of selflessness, or work with the poor. He simply wants to embrace me, my brokenness, and my heart. We don't need to put on a pretend happy face or sing and dance and skip our way through hard times. Praising God for Who He is when praising is hard is the true meaning of a sacrifice of praise.

God wants a faithful love that lasts, not more fake religion. He wants people to know Him. (Hosea 6:6, Matthew 9:13).

Reflection: What's On My Heart?

Has your miscarriage burdened and broken you beyond your strength? Can you trust the promise of Isaiah 41:10, NASB? *"Do not fear, for I am with you. Do not be afraid, for I am your God. I will strengthen you, I will also help you, I will also uphold you with My righteous right hand."*

List the fears or worries you will trust God to provide the strength and help to overcome.

Reread Isaiah 41:10, then praise God for what He promises He will do for you.

I don't know what the future holds for any of us. Even though this book nears an end, our stories continue to be written one character at a time. Write with flavor. Write with passion. Better yet, if you want to be freaked out most of the time, place the pen in the Author's hands. He is, after all, the author of the greatest action-suspense-love story ever written.

In the Words of Others

Dear Mom,

I know. I just know. This sucks. After three years of infertility, I get it. I've been there.

I heard my baby Phillip cry once. He took one breath on earth and left for heaven. Doctors told me later, his twin brother, Querubin, hadn't survived past 12 weeks.

I was teaching ESL first grade in Saigon, Saipan, Vietnam CNMI at the time, so not only was I isolated in my grief, I was also separated from friends and family by a hemisphere. "Lonely" doesn't cut what I felt.

The week after we lost our sons, my husband Alex and I sought solace at Catholic mass. In Vietnam, children roam free during worship. Children run, laugh, and grin with bright, white smiles and shout, "Mom! Mom!"

"Nope. Not happening."

Our butts had barely warmed the seats when I melted into a blubbering mess. "Alex, can we go?" We stood up and walked out.

Worship hurt. I don't remember returning to Mass before returning to the States.

God took three children from me, back to back. The losses didn't cause me to lose faith in God, but when I finally could worship, loving Him came with a cost.

I knew God loved me. I also believed God was gonna do what God was gonna do. He had a crazy, messed up plan and I could only watch what would happen next.

"God, you already have three of my babies. Can I please have one on earth now?"

Because of my past, our daughter we conceived was considered high-risk. The closest hospital to perform the frequent in-depth ultrasounds was nearly two hours away.

After three years of infertility, God gave us one low-maintenance pregnancy daughter. After Clomid treatments, we birthed another son and conceived his brother, who nearly died in NICU, six months later.

Don't pressure yourself to return to church too soon. Don't think less of yourself if you can't immediately praise the God who didn't save your baby.

God loves you even if you don't love Him back. And when you do finally worship again, your offering will be precious and sweet, because it will come from a place of brokenness within you.

Hang in there, woman. You've got this.

Love,

Angie

Heal

Heed: Rejoice and Blossom

The desert and the parched land will be glad;
the wilderness will rejoice and blossom.
Like the crocus, it will burst into bloom;
it will rejoice greatly and shout for joy.
The glory of Lebanon will be given to it,
the splendor of Carmel and Sharon;
they will see the glory of the Lord,
the splendor of our God.

Exhale Fear: Inhale God's Strength

Strengthen the feeble hands,
steady the knees that give way;
say to those with fearful hearts,
"Be strong, do not fear;
your God will come,
he will come with vengeance;
with divine retribution
he will come to save you."

Acknowledge: The Way of Holiness

Then will the eyes of the blind be opened
and the ears of the deaf unstopped.
Then will the lame leap like a deer,
and the mute tongue shout for joy.
Water will gush forth in the wilderness
and streams in the desert.
The burning sand will become a pool,
the thirsty ground bubbling springs.
In the haunts where jackals once lay,
grass and reeds and papyrus will grow.
And a highway will be there;
it will be called the Way of Holiness;
it will be for those who walk on that Way.
. . . only the redeemed will walk there,
and those the Lord has rescued will return.

Lighten Your Load: The Sacrifice of Praise

They will enter Zion with singing;
everlasting joy will crown their heads.
Gladness and joy will overtake them,
and sorrow and sighing will flee away.
Isaiah 35:1–8; 10, NIV

23 Unexpected Ending

After I miscarried my first baby, I typed my first messy manuscript. As the cursor hovered over the "Send" button, I hesitated. Clint sat across the room, zombified by a football game on TV.

"Clint, if I hit 'Send,' the whole world will have access to my vagina." I felt vulnerable at the thought of lobbing my story into cyberspace.

Clint didn't respond to what I believed was a witty metaphor. Eyes vacant, Clint might as well have had drool dripping from his slackened jaw.

With little ceremony, save in my own mind, I published *Love Letters to Miscarried Moms*, which I wrote within the whirlwind of my loss, so you would not be alone in yours. For your sake, and for the thousands of women who read my book, I'm grateful I published my story.

For your sake, I thank God for my miscarriages. I prayed for you and cried with you. My heart has torn with you. Your journey toward healing was worth my pain.

As I hoped, my life changed. I'm the mother of (God's Child #1), (God's Child #2), Kaylynn, Kelly, (God's Child #3), and Trinity.

You'd think I'd get the hang of the unforeseen situations by now. Little did I realize that I'd face an even greater challenge that called upon the lessons learned about grieving and resilience from my miscarriages.

October 1, Sunday morning, 1:30 a.m.: "Mrs. Evans, there's been an accident."

Sunday morning, 7:45 a.m.: I calculated the time required to bathe, dress, and feed our three daughters aged six, five, and three years old for church. I rehearsed the announcement and rolled over details needed to officiate the church service. Conditioner in my hair. The phone rang.

"Mrs. Evans. This is the hospital. We found something on the CT scan. You need to come in right away. Don't bring your children."

The diagnosis? Stage IV cancer.

October 2, Monday morning: "Methodist Pastor Arrested for Drunk Driving" splayed across the front page news, including my husband's mug shot.

Late January, 16 months later: The truth of Clint's diagnosis seemed no more real.

Marble pillars stretched toward the vaulted ceiling. Intricate paintings depicting the Stations of the Cross, also known as the Way of Sorrows, wrapped around the dimly lit sanctuary.

I chose a pew far away from the other women on the retreat. One by one, each woman approached the spiritual director for prayer while I selfishly waited to speak to her last.

Clint's drunk-driving accident, and the means by which we discovered the cancer, had happened

16 months prior. The memories collided with one another like breakers upon the rocks, trapping my mind in the undertow.

The spiritual director invited herself into my pew and I rested my head on her lap. "Hey, Stef."

She stroked my hair. "I'd ask how you're doing, but that's a stupid question." Together we wept about Clint's diagnosis.

"I feel like I'm suffocating." I closed my eyes and described how I felt—frightened, burdened, overwhelmed. Somewhere along the way, another person highjacked my thoughts.

I can't breathe. I can't breathe.

I'm Peter in the boat, straining to see Jesus through the storm. I hurtle myself from the boat with enough faith to walk on water. After all, Peter did. Raindrops slash the darkness and pelt my face.

"Where are you, Jesus? Where did you go?"

Lightening streaks across a violet, violent sky. My toes trip on a wave. My knees buckle.

Water engulfs me. I strain toward the surface, clawing at currents pouring through my fingers. Darkness spins, swallowing me on all sides.

Jesus?

I question my Lord with the last of my fading light.

Jesus.

I disappear.

Lifeless, my limbs float on the whim of the windswept water.

Void.

Concerted strength punches my chest. The rhythmic pressure resounds as if a timpani reverberates throughout my hollow body.

Warm lips meet my cold-and-grayed ones.

My lungs inflate with someone's breath. Heat races toward each extremity. Life floods through me; washes over me.

My senses switch on one at a time.

Smell—briny, fishy murky. The smell rolls into my mouth. Bitter, nauseous.

Thunder resounds overhead. The rumbling distorted, muted somehow.

Water laps against my limbs and ripples beneath me.

Peace trickles down and infiltrates the marrow of my bones.

My eyes flutter open.

Droplets clinging to my lashes obscure my vision, but Jesus' profile against the raging sky is unmistakable.

Jesus kneels beside me. Though He is near, He has not calmed the storm.

Confusion parts like clouds.

I lay atop the sea as if the waves are a mattress. I touch my fingers to my lips. Recognition dawns.

CPR.

Jesus resuscitated me, reviving me from death.

No! I catapult to my feet. No! Not me! Him!

I spin in every direction searching for Clint. Though I can't see my husband through the blasted rain, I know he's out there, facing the same storm. Clint is stronger than me, but his strength wanes.

Not me! Go to Clint! Jesus, please save him!

Why me? Why not him?

Guilt drags me down like an anchor. I betrayed

Clint by stealing the sustaining breath he needs! He's the one with cancer, not me.

Tears of desperation spring from my eyes. If the choice must be between him and me, choose him.

Please choose him. I'll give anything.

I feel the drag—the pressure of water rushing past my face as I'm lifted from the depths.

Surfacing from the vision, I stared up at Stef. Her hand stilled in my hair. Her eyes and face were as drenched as mine. Everything I saw, I spoke out loud—about my husband; her close friend, colleague, and confidant.

I raised my head from her lap, expelling a shuddered breath. She reached for the tissue box. My heart steadied—as if I'd found my resting heart rate following an intense race. We sat beside one another in instant calm—what I now know was the eye of the storm.

For several minutes, neither of us spoke. The only sound was obnoxious amounts of snot blown into tissue after tissue.

Six months later, Clint died in June.

Dear Clint,

It's been 16 months since you died. Our daughters, our three precious little girls, deserve, and need so much more than this shell of a human who struggles even to keep them fed and bathed.

Every day's color is the same barren brown— like autumn after all the trees shed their leaves and the bite in the air promises impending snow. For months, I've resided in the Valley of the

Shadow of Death where I stumble among lifeless bones. Little difference exists between those whose breath vanished ages ago and myself. I trudge like a zombie through this bleak world, carelessly tripping on the bones of the dead.

I don't recognize the life I'm living without you. I don't recognize myself without you as my mirror, reflecting back at me.

Where am I? How did I come to this place? God's vibrant blessings surround me beyond measure, but the colors of blessings are muted— the enjoyment of them beyond my reach. This is not a life, but the mere shadow of one, the echoes of a past I reach for, but will never grasp. These dusty skeletons know my story more intimately than the living do.

My body aged with your death. I felt stiffness in my joints that was not there before. My spiritual and emotional atrophy led to a physical disintegration. I am not far behind the bones beneath my feet.

Lost and Wandering,
Sam

Dear Sam,[1]

You and I trudged through plenty of deserts together, didn't we? The miscarriages, my stupid addictions. Life hasn't been easy. This time is harder for you, because I'm not there to walk alongside you. And I know you feel like you're alone, so alone, but you're not. I'm right here.

---

1 Some letters attributed to Clint in this chapter are based on sermons Clint wrote and shared in our church. Other letters are based on a journal I kept following Clint's death, in which I imagined how Clint would respond to my heartache.

You're not losing me. How could you, sweetheart, when you will always hold my heart?

And Jesus is closer to you than a breath.

You can't talk about dry bones around Jesus, as if lifelessness means anything. You know that right? The Dude raised up about 230 square miles of Thomas Deadisons, Humphrey Bonegarts and Scary Poppinses. God specializes in raising the dead, so if you feel like a zombie, He can work with that.

And there's no pressure, Sam. He gets it. He gets how hard this is for you. He could have saved me, yet He chose not to. And you're the one at the raw end of that deal, so you just stay silent as long as it takes. Even though I wonder why you were never quite this quiet when I was alive.

It's okay, Sam. It's gonna be all right.

There's a reason, Sweetheart, why within seven verses the words "breath" or "breathe" are used seven times. (Ezekiel 37:4–10) God makes the point that not only did He breathe life into them, He never left them in the first place. God is as near to them as their own breath, even through their trials. So even though Israel remained in exile for decades, Ezekiel promises Israel, "The LORD will place His Spirit within you and you will live." (Ezekiel 37:5–6, 9)

Even Israel, God's chosen people said, "Our bones are dried up and our hope is gone; we are cut off."

God's reply through Ezekiel?

> *"I will make breath enter you, and you will come to life. My people, I am going to open your graves and bring*

*you up from them; I will bring you
back to the land of Israel. Then you,
my people, will know that I am the
LORD, when I open your graves and
bring you up from them. I will put my
Spirit in you and you will live, and I
will settle you in your own land. Then
you will know that I the LORD have
spoken, and I have done it, declares
the LORD,'"* Ezekiel 37:5, 11–14, NIV.

God's breath sustains us. But then again, you already knew that, didn't you? You've received his breath before.

Dear Sam,

You forgot about the vision, didn't you? You needed Stef to help you remember. Good 'ol Stef. Love me some Morgans. I understand why you couldn't remember the vision. You felt so guilty for receiving the sustaining breath that might have saved me; you felt like you betrayed me. That, and you knew what God told you, but you didn't want to hear it. You weren't ready to hear it.

You knew that I wouldn't need to be sustained, but after my death, you would. Jesus tried to tell you that I was going to die. Jesus didn't calm the storm in your vision. He only gave you strength to survive the waves. And this was the time, Sweetheart, the moment He knew you needed Him.

It breaks my heart to see you keeping God at arm's length. Maybe you think God should have given you preferential treatment, but it doesn't work that way. You can't equate God's love for you with a lack of suffering. I get it though. Mary and Martha, Jesus' close friends, struggled with the same thing.

They witnessed and heard of his miracles. When they sent Jesus the message, "Lord, our brother, the one whom you love is sick," the sisters waited in eager expectation for their close family friend, Jesus to come. (John 11:3) Of course, Jesus would heal His friend and their brother.

We know Jesus received the word, but in obedience to the Father waited two days before traveling back home.

Meanwhile, Lazarus grew sicker. His breath faded. His heart slowed. These are details I wish you didn't have intimate knowledge of. I can still feel the place where your hand rested over my heart as you simultaneously consoled yourself with its beating and pled for God to stop my pulse to spare my agony. Do you know how brave you are?

Anyway, I can picture Mary and Martha pacing, taking turns looking anxiously out the window.

"Is he here yet? Do you see him?"

"No. You sent the message, right?"

"Yes, of course."

As tensions rose, I bet they even argued.

But Jesus was a no show and Lazarus died.

Four days later, Jesus finally showed up. The sisters didn't notice the heaviness in His gait.

Martha said, "Lord, if you had been here, my brother would not have died, but I know that even now, God will give you whatever you ask." (John 11:21–22)

Mary bolted toward Jesus, desperate for the comfort of her friend, and fell at his feet. Jesus was *"deeply moved in spirit."* (John 11:33) And then we arrive at one of the most well-known verses in the Bible:

"Jesus wept," John 11:35, NASB.

Wept—a deep, emotional response—not the shedding of one or two tears—an abundance of tears.

Jesus sobbed along with Mary. Seeing people suffer pained Jesus. I bet the two days He waited absolutely killed him inside.

But the people needed to see that no matter what, God overcomes all—even death.

You say, "That's a great story, Clinty Evans, but you're still dead."

Correct. And so is Lazarus. So are all the other people Jesus healed. All the disciples are dead, too. Jesus' disciples, who were brutally killed for their beliefs, were beheaded, crucified, dragged, stabbed, stoned, clubbed, skinned alive, and burned. No preferential treatment there.

Jesus' healings are only a foretaste of what will happen when Jesus returns. And, Sam, Jesus will come back—not just to escort us to heaven one at a time as you witnessed, but in unleashed, blazing glory.

Our God is not just a God who watches from the distance, He suffers alongside us. So, despite what you're going through, please embrace hope.

I love you. You know that, right? I know you're in the midst of a desert right now. I can tell because you're not writing as much as you used to. Writing is the litmus test for Sam Evans' well-being. I wish I could remove this hardship from you, but I don't possess that power. Don't look at me like that.

Yes, God holds that omnipotent power. No, He didn't give you what you wanted. How long will you carry your anger toward Him? Suck it up, Buttercup. You're a force to be reckoned with and grief only amplifies your fierceness. It's time to pick up your pen.

✐〜✐

Dear Clint,

Once upon a time, writing siphoned the creative spirit within until my authenticity and humor bled onto the page. I felt a connection to God through writing and His inspiration as I typed:

> *"He must increase, but I must decrease,"*
> John 3:30, NASB.

The finished product surprised me as much as it did my readers.

I took for granted the months and years I spent tuned into the Father's melody without effort. Stepping into that secret place with our Savior for writing's sake hurt me. Bridging the stretched silence between us singed my soul.

I can't outrun the grief. The fury within me hums beneath my skin like an electrical current. I dug out a fire pit. I planted bushels of flowers beneath the scorching sun. For weeks, I hauled rock, cleared dead branches, and hefted dirt. I climbed atop the roof with a neighbor and cleared low-hanging branches away from the house. Still, my fury was not spent.

I pounded my body into submission with HIIT workouts until my arches screamed. My knee declared mutiny. I swam lung busters in a pool until I could no longer breathe. Still the fury remained.

No amount of words I type will erase the pain within me. And writing, for me, acts like a speed dial to the Spirit. A lightening rod. Tapping into my writing talent is an act of obedience and total surrender. I'm terrified to type, to drop beneath the surface of my grief.

Yet, I know as deeply as I know that God loves me, I will not truly heal until every last word within me is spent onto a page. Writing, purging, pouring out my heart, will overflow every floodgate in the dam holding my grief at bay.

I trust that God's Ephesians 3:18 *agape* is greater than the outpouring of my grief. However, I suspect in my limited capacity, pound for pound, God's Grace v. My Grief will feel like a pretty even matchup and my heart is the ground zero for collateral damage. I'm in no hurry for the floodwaters to test the God-strength within.

So, am I writing? No. I am not. Not truly. Because I know what will happen when I do.

Evans out.

Sam,

Don't "Evans out" me. I gave you that last name.

One of the hardest things about being a Christian is that we are called to give full control over to God. This includes time, which means we rely on God's time and wait on God's timing.

I asked you in the hospital, "Sam, why won't He take me yet?" I only waited 13 days from the moment I surrendered into the pain and those minutes still felt like forever.

The Desert Song spoke to us when we miscarried. Do you remember? Jill McCloghry wrote that song after her newborn son died.

After the Casting Crowns band members met a little girl with a tremendous faith despite her cancer diagnosis, they wrote *Praise You in this Storm*. She's home here with the Lord. I think it's impossible not to question God's timing in situations like that.

Jill allowed God to make something beautiful out of that tragedy that's impacted many lives. Casting Crowns honored a little girl with a great big faith. You and I have the same opportunity.

I've always believed in your writing, Sam. You're an amazing storyteller. I also think it's hilarious that you gauge the success of your writing upon whether or not your readers laugh or cry. You've changed thousands of lives with your book and I know, whenever you're ready, your next book will rock the house.

But you need to let God have His way with you again. People have always been, will always be, attracted to you because you carry His Spirit within you and acknowledge the grace He bestows upon you. Your writing is high caliber because you allow God to use you and to speak through you. You're an Ezekiel.

You are loved, Sam, so, so loved. As it has always been for you, let His grace be sufficient.

With All His Love, I Agape You.

Clint

Friends, when life gets really difficult, don't jump to the conclusion that God isn't on the job. Instead, be glad that you are in the very thick of what Christ experienced. This is a spiritual refining process, with glory just around the corner.

1 Peter 4:12-13.

MSG

Dear Clint,

It feels so good to hear your voice. I wish that this were real. The storm has finally passed. I feel like the sole survivor of my shipwrecked life. You died 16 months ago. Now, in this calm after the storm, I feel Jesus' presence mere feet away, as if He sits on the couch to my right as I write. He doesn't speak.

Your victory is my tragedy—I must come to terms with this truth. Jesus knows there's nothing left to say. And still, His breath fortifies me. A peace that passes all understanding soothes the aches within the marrow of my bones.

I'm still in the desert, but God has brought me up from the grave and called me by name. I will follow Him home.

Love you still,

Wifeykins

Lord Jesus,

Fill me with your Spirit and sustaining breath. It's time to write again.

> *Then Job replied to the LORD:*
> *"I know that you can do all things;*
> *no purpose of yours can be thwarted.*
> *You asked, 'Who is this that obscures my*
> *plans without knowledge?'*
> *Surely I spoke of things I did not*
> *understand,*
> *things too wonderful for me to know.*
> *"You said, 'Listen now, and I will speak;*
> *I will question you,*

and you shall answer me.'
My ears had heard of you
but now my eyes have seen you.
Therefore I despise myself
and repent in dust and ashes."

Dear Sam,[2]

"*The desert and the parched land will be glad; the wilderness will rejoice and blossom. Like the crocus, which grows despite colder temperatures, it will burst into bloom; it will rejoice greatly and shout for joy,*" Isaiah 35:1–2, NIV.

I know we've been through hell and I'm so sorry. My constant prayer and praise is that something beautiful comes from this wilderness. I love you more than words can express.

Love Always,
Clinty Evans

We have all these great people around us as examples. Their lives tell us what faith means. So we, too, should run the race that is before us and never quit. We should remove from our lives anything that would slow us down.

We must never stop looking to Jesus, the leader of our faith, who makes our faith complete.

Hebrews 12:1-3, ERV

---

2 Taken from a card Clint gave Sam two years before his death.

Reflection: What's On My Heart?

When I think about tragedy and loss, I believe God loves me deeply and will not distance Himself from me. God mourns alongside me as only His inexhaustive love can. Throughout the mourning journey, God's restoration power penetrates the darkness of my grief. His Son, who also died on a cross, also bore the burden of all my pain and the pain of every person. Jesus also wept over the death of his friend Lazarus.

Jesus' sacrificial death and triumphant resurrection defeated death and I'm comforted that I'll be reunited with my loved ones for eternity. My tragedies inked in this book are blurred blessings in disguise. As God wipes away every tear I shed, I pray my words offer the gift of comfort and will wipe away your precious tears.

My experience with mourning has taught me . . .

In the Words of Others

Dear Sam,

Thanks for your message. I cried when I read, "I take your loss personally. I would have stood in front of you for anything, so I feel like God should have protected you from miscarriage. I'm mad at Him for you." I also read between the lines, "You idiot, why didn't you call me sooner?"

I remember in high school, finishing track practice after I spent an hour running sprints, and seeing you start your 12 laps around the track. I joined you, running backwards and taunting you. You looked like you were about to suffocate, and I told you your workout would be "a nice cool down." Every time I saw you at the track that spring, I ran with you. And when you PR'ed at the 5K in June, you said, sarcastically, it's because I paced you.

My heart broke with yours when you and Clint lost your baby. But I watched the two of you with awe as you rose from the ashes—literally. (How many youth directors build a shed for a play just so their teens can burn it down?)

I don't know why it took me so long to tell you about our miscarriages—the words are hard to articulate. The losses devastated me, but for Danielle, the pain seemed ten times worse.

Then we received your book in the mail and read it together. I did the math as we read—you lost another baby while you directed us in "The Best Christmas Pageant Ever," and we never knew.

You say back then I pulled you from the fire, I paced you. But Sam, you paced Danielle and I in our grief. For the first time, she felt like someone understood, like she wasn't alone.

You stood in front of us, between the fire and us, and I'm not quite sure how to thank you for that.

Your Friend,

Levi

The Gardener and the Phoenix

I've foolishly believed time and again
That I author my life, that I hold the pen.
Life to the fullest God wanted for me,
So I contrived and I scribbled and I wrote fervently.
But the stories never ended the way I planned
Tragedies invaded the script in my hand.

Outside in the garden, I threw my effort to the fire,
My hopes and my dreams and all I aspired.
With the weighted knowledge
Life would ne'er be the same
I watched dark smoke chortle up from the flames.

I awoke the next morning, drenched in grief
Empty of tears, but starved of relief.
I peeked out the window to witness the dawn of new day
And saw a form near the ashes through vanishing haze.

The Gardener crouched, with moisture in his eyes
And scattered the ashes as He silently cried.
Then I heard Him speaking into the still
His voice, hands, heart manifested His will.
His tears landed like crystal seeds
And where each drop fell, a sprout conceived.
He patted the soil with gentle grace
And from the ashes, beauty rose in its place

SAMANTHA EVANS

He lowered himself against a tree.
Withdrawing parchment and ink,
He scrawled against his knees.
Not simply a gardener, I realized,
The Creator, Redeemer, the Author of Life.

I rushed to the garden. I knelt at His feet.
I surrendered the pen I'd been tempted to keep.
"Write me broken, devastated, scared, and confused.
Write me lonely, battered, exhausted, and bruised."

He laughed at my request, which I didn't expect
And laid aside His story to straighten the facts.
"I'll write you bold, brave, strong, artistic, and kind.
I'll write you tender, steadfast, generous, and wise.
Battle-scarred, perhaps, but as always with us
Blessing awaits on this side of trust."

I stared over His shoulder at the illustration He drew.
Glorious, exquisite, blazing brawn.
"Tragedy with my ink is blessing blurred in disguise.
I've depicted you as a phoenix.
From these ashes we'll rise."
1.27.20

About Samantha Evans

Samantha Evans, author of the award-winning *Love Letters to Miscarriage moms,* updated her book and entitled the second edition *Love Letters to Miscarriage Moms: You Are Not Alone.* After the original publication in 2011, Clint and Sam Evans' family grew, totaling three heaven-born babies and three beautiful, earth-born daughters.

Evans co-authored three versions of *Adventure Devos* with writer, photographer, certified white-water rafter, and hang-from-mountain-upside-downer, Eric Sprinkle. In 2018, Evans won back-to-back "Writer of the Month" awards through Good Catch Publishing (GCP). Her freelance work through GCP consisted of interviewing people about their God stories and writing those stories in first person.

In June of 2019, Evans' husband Clint joined their heaven-borns after a 20-month battle with cancer. Clint died four months before anyone uttered, "COVID-19." During quarantine, Evans contributed to multiple anthologies by DaySpring.

As with *Love Letters*, in the upcoming release of *The Rocky Path of Grief: Navigating the Loss of a Loved One,* Evans continues to share the truth with humor, transparency, and love. In the midst of her grief and loss, Sam conveys the most important message of all: You are worthy of God's love.

Acknowledgments: Meet the Cast and Crew

I'd like to thank those who guided me through my darkness by gifting me with their stories and their time. While all our details differ, the loss is similar. This book would not have been the same without those who laughed and wept with me, and those who shared their stories and their letters written to you. "God's Child" refers to a miscarried or stillborn child who entered into heaven and lives in God's presence.

The Cast Who Walked Alongside Me During my Miscarriages

The following friends and family members celebrated the joy of my pregnancy and affirmed the hurt of my loss.

Lona: Mother of three children on earth and twins in heaven. Her sharp, unexpected humor triggered my first laughter following my miscarriage.

Annie: Mother of two beautiful girls with another on the way.

Sonia and her child's father served together in the National Guard. While serving in Iraq, she got pregnant and miscarried during a hospital visit with a friend in labor.

Dia: Mother of God's Child #1, Iollia, Naida, D.J., God's Child #2, God's Child #3, God's Child #4 (D.J.), Malinna Enarra, God's Child #5, God's Child #6, God's Child #7/8—twins, God's Child #9 (J.D.), Zinnia, Azizza, Petra, God's Child #9, God's Child #10, God's Child #11, God's Child #12, and God's Child #13. Dia and her husband, Dana, nicknamed our child 'Little Clam'—a moniker for Clint and Sam.

Dr. Gwenn: When I was sick without insurance, she examined me in the men's Sunday school classroom after church. She and her husband Mike go back as far as my memories do. Mike and Gwenn are the parents of Matt, God's Child #1, and God's Child #2. Gwenn is now a grandmother.

Dr. Mary: At the time of her miscarriage, her job would never have made accommodations for her to raise her children. My family doctor, reflected, "Looking back, I realize the timing wasn't right for a baby." After her miscarriage Mary and her husband re-evaluated their lifestyle. Dr. Mary is the mother of God's Child #1, Connor, Cameron, and Elizabeth.

Erica: I marveled at Erica's patience, our church Administrative Assistant, with the chaos of our church. Erica and Coe are the parents of God's Child #1, Payton, and Cade. She claims her sons provide the source of her patience.

Diane: Mother of God's Child #1, God's Child #2, and God's Child #3.

Jenny: Miscarried around Thanksgiving and I recall thinking, *Oh, that's too bad.* I never fathomed her pain until I experienced my miscarriage. Jenny and Jarred are the parents of Jacob, Christiana, Caroline Chevelle, God's Child #1,

Charlotte Mae, Claire, and Joshua. Recovering from the loss of Jenny's fourth child proved difficult. Even before her miscarriage, she turned around in a store, counted three children and wondered, *Where's the fourth child?*

Lori: A sign hanging in Lori's house reads: "There are four seasons in this house: Winter, Spring, Summer, and Football." Lori and Mike are parents of God's Child #1, Steven, Alex, and Sam. She loves her crazy busy life. The first and second day after I miscarried, Lori made time for me, which I now realize was a special gift. Lori is now a grandmother.

Mary Beth: An oncology nurse, Mary Beth is the mother of Christy, Carissa, Melissa, God's Child #1, Cheryl, God's Child #2, and Robert. Mary's first miscarriage happened in the first trimester. Her second loss was a still-birth at five months.

Misty: Misty has a beautiful heart and a beautiful voice. Before I peed on the stick, she learned I was the same age as her oldest son. She announced, "I'll be your surrogate mom." The day I miscarried she left for vacation, but promised, "When I return, I'll spoil you rotten." After I miscarried, my mom said, "I wish I could be closer to you." When I told her about Misty, she said, "Oh, good, I'm glad. That makes me feel better." Misty and Jeff are parents of God's Child #1, Steven, Jarred, and Julian.

Monica: Monica and Nat are parents of Addison, Christian, Beth, Titus, Sidney, Cadence, God's Child #1, Eva, and Sophia. Their household exudes energy. Titus sprinted up to me, flexed his four-year-old biceps and declared, "I'm a strong little buddy. My Tigger says so." At five years old, he stuck rubber handled pliers into the electrical outlet and yelled, "Mommy, Look! Fireworks!" Monica laughed too hard to scold him. I want their energy in my life—maybe not eight kids worth—but since my miscarriage our home is emptier than before.

Sandie: Mother of God's Child #1, God's Child #2, God's Child #3. We bonded as instant friends when we learned we shared the same birthday. Like a cross between Betty Crocker and McGuiver, Sandie can do anything she sets her mind to. With the tenacity required to pull off any project started, the inability to bear children was difficult and, she questioned, "Why am I not good enough?"

The Crew Who Wrote Letters and Shared their Hearts

Amanda: Mother of Bryson, Clayton, God's Child #1, and Abigail.

Andrea: Mother of Paige, Mark, God's Child #1, and Daniel.

Angie: Mother of Philip, God's Child #1, Querubin, God's Child #2, God's Child #3, Lexanna, Carter, and Clark.

Anonymous: Those who preferred to remain anonymous, thank you.

Bev: Mother of Reagan and Brady.

Danielle and Levi: Parents of one child in heaven and two on earth.

Darci: Mother of Hannah, Elizabeth, Leah, God's Child #1, and Matthew.

Erin: Mother of five children—three in heaven and two on earth.

John: Father of Adam, God's Child #1, Ryan, Madalyn.

LeAnna: Mother of God's Child #1, William, Norah, and God's Child #2.

Madison: Mother of Peanut, God's Child #1, Sawyer, and Rio.

Sandie: Mother of God's Child #1 and #2—twins, God's Child #3, and God's Child #4.

Scoti: Mother of God's Child #1, Kristoffer, an Army Ranger, who was killed in Afghanistan on his 14th deployment, and Kyle.

Stef: Mother of Zoey, Zander, Sophia, and God's Child #1.

Tom and Julee: Tom and Julee live in Indiana and are the parents of God's Child #1, Tommy, and Becca.

Appendix
Helpful Tips on How to Support Someone Who Experienced a Miscarriage

In college, friends kidded I should come with a manual, so I wrote one entitled, *Helpful Tips on How to Manage a Sam.* I constructed the covers with cardboard, hole-punched the cover and pages, and tied the book together with twisty ties.

Grievers should also come with a manual. For those who've never experienced grief, the following insights may help your efforts to love your friend, sister, daughter, or niece more effectively.

My first week after the miscarriage was the hardest. On a beautiful, bright sunny day, I felt numb and detached. Valerie, a mom-friend who never miscarried, became for me the hands and feet of Jesus. I received a text from Valerie:

Valerie: What do you need right now?

My response to her was the first text I attempted since dropping my phone into the fire. I contemplated explaining the fire story to her, but the tale required far too much effort.

Sam: I just need to stop crying right now.
Valerie: Can I bring you dinner?

I didn't respond. I was too busy crying and typing a response required far too much thumb strength on the bubbled keypad.

Valerie: I'm bringing you dinner.

And did she ever. Lasagna that she baked before coming over, salad, dressing, garlic bread, and chocolate ice cream, so I could make a chocolate peanut butter shake for dessert. Attached to the dinner, she left a note card that read, "God is with you . . . May His love be soothing. May His words bring you strength. May His promise fill your heart with His peace. With deepest sympathy to you at this time of sorrow. Sam and Clint, we love you both and are praying for you. God's love never fails! In Christ, Kyle & Valerie."

Provide Food

Food is good. If you can't cook, send a pizza to your friend's house. Order a meal from her favorite restaurant and have DoorDash or GrubHub deliver it to her front door. Or buy rotisserie chicken, potato salad, and fruit. Providing a meal will make all the difference in the world.

Know Your Girl

I loved cards in the mail, friends stopping by. I hated text messages because they felt super impersonal. As an extreme extrovert, I shared many details with many people to process my pain.

My friend Abby only wanted to talk to her husband about the miscarriage and no one else. Every time a friend or family member brought up her miscarriages, she felt like she was losing the baby all over again.

Moms who miscarried compiled the following list. As you read through these suggestions, remember, every woman is different. You're the batter up in a no-win situation. Nothing you say can erase her grief, but showing her you care is vital.

- Acknowledge her loss.
- Realize her child died.
- Say, "I love you. I'm sorry. I'm in your corner."
- Choose your words carefully.
- Be gentle with her frail heart.
- Say, "I'm so sorry. I can't imagine what you're feeling."
- Remind her you care. "I'm praying for you."
- Provide practical support.
- Paint her nails or pay for a manicure or massage.

Say what you mean and mean what you say. If you say, "Maybe I'll stop by," stop by. Be the same friend you've always been. Do you usually barge in on her? Yes or no? Miscarriage rocked her world, so status quo when possible provides unspoken reassurance.

Does she have other children? Schedule a night to watch her children so she and her husband can get out of the house.

Say, "Hey, I saw [unicorns running in a field today] which made me think of you. How are you doing?"

Treat love as a verb through acts of kindness.

Send Flowers, Cards, Notes, or Texts

Six years after my Aunt Thelma lost my Uncle Ron, we received a card from her in the mail. "I've never experienced miscarriage myself, so I don't know how you feel, but I know loss hurts." Even though she lost a spouse, she didn't pretend to understand. "Of one thing I'm sure—Uncle Ron is rocking your little one and will do so until you get there."

Understand that you'll forget about someone's miscarriage long before she does. If you're still thinking of her loss, there's still time to take her out to dinner, buy flowers, or send a card.

Just when a mother thinks she's moving forward through her grief, she'll hit her due date, Mother's Day, or the anniversary of the miscarriage.

Acknowledge that she's a mother on Mother's Day, even if her experience as a mom differs from yours. On Mother's Day, send a card or text her. "I remember and know this day is painful. I love you and am praying for you and your husband. Can I bring you your favorite chocolate, or red or white wine, or sparkling grape juice, or all of the aforementioned?"

Social Media Miscarriage Etiquette

Don't post on social media about someone's miscarriage. Respect her privacy. A miscarriage is the mother's story to tell, not yours.

If someone other than the mom shares the news with you, message her. Don't post a public response.

If the mom announces the loss of their child on social media and you don't know what to say, acknowledge the loss with a concerned or tears emoji. No words are better than posting a cliché. Or simply say, "I'm so sorry for your loss."

Avoid Cliché's that Ignite Lava-like Fury

- "At least you weren't [time frame] along."
- "I know how you feel."
- "You're young. You'll get pregnant again."
- "Oh, it wasn't meant to be."

- "Oh, you can have another one." Another child can't replace the loss of a child.
- "At least you already have a kid." If one of your children died, would you say, "at least we still have Johnny?"
- "Miscarriage is really common."
- "My friend had a miscarriage and . . . "
- "It's for the best."
- "Everything happens for a reason."
- "How far along were you?"
- "[Insert Name] miscarriage was worse than yours."
- "You're lucky, kids are so stressful."
- "You'll get over it. Time heals all wounds."
- "It's God's will."

Avoid Unsolicited Advice that Blames or Guilt's the Mom

- "Maybe you shouldn't have worked so hard."
- "You were too stressed out."
- "Stop overthinking your miscarriage."

Avoid 'Helpful' Advice

- "Maybe you should take a vacation."
- "When do you plan to try again?"
- "Maybe you should take some time and just relax."

Listen and Mirror

Mirroring and listening may sound absurdly simple, but the concept is important to understand. Create rapport by watching and mirroring her verbal and nonverbal behavior: Tune into to her voice and words and observe her gestures, posture, and other non-verbal cues.

- Allow her to grieve and to vent her loss.
- Don't pretend to understand what she's going through. Unless you experienced the death of a child, sibling, or spouse, you will not even come close to understanding her pain. Even then, each person experiences grief in a different way.
- Allow the grieving woman to set the tone of the conversation. Study her

facial expressions and gestures. If she keeps the conversation light, keep the conversation light.

- Ask open-ended questions like, "How's your day been?" Or "What have you been up to today?"
- Cry when she cries.
- Laugh when she laughs.

To Hug or Not to Hug

If she doesn't reach out her arms to hug you, please don't envelop her and pull her into a hug. Not everyone likes to be hugged. If she looks like she's about to melt to the floor in a weepy puddle, then embrace the poor woman— or ask her if you can.

The week after I miscarried, I didn't want to be touched by many people. Still bleeding, I felt dirty and nasty. My emotional stability clung by a thread. I feared if someone hugged me, I'd shatter into unfixable pieces.

Another couple turned my news of the miscarriage into a group hug. I said, "Okay, that's enough hugging," as I wrestled my way out of their embrace.

This behavior may sound selfish to you, but how a miscarriage mom mourns belongs to her. She's allowed to respond however she needs to. For now, this is a one-way street and you need to respond however she needs you to.

Don't Hijack Her Mourning or Make Her Loss about You

About a month after my miscarriage, work details preoccupied me. For several blissful hours, I forgot I miscarried.

A woman entered the office, stared at me with puppy eyes on the verge of tears and said, "I need to apologize to you."

"For what?" I asked. *Oh no, not that.* I lifted my arm parallel to the floor with my palm facing out in a "Stop in the name of love" fashion and stated, "I don't want to be hugged right now." She ignored my request.

I found myself embracing this sobbing woman, rubbing her back, and consoling her over my loss. While she never said so, I suspect this woman wept over her own miscarriage(s). Still, the exchange was inappropriate.

Never Forget

Every miscarriage mother works through grief on her timetable. She's a mother who lost her child. She planned for a future that will never come.

She brainstormed names and imagined whether her child would be athletic or artsy, spunky, or subdued.

She wondered, *Will my child share my brilliant looks or inherit Daddy's amazing eyes?*

If you think the loss is less severe because the child was never born—you're wrong. By believing this, you demean the extent of her grief and undermine her recovery.

As I type "I miss my baby so much," tears stream down my face. My loss wasn't just an embryo or a fetus. I carried a human within me, my baby. And my child vanished. Because my heart was broken, I know your friend's heart is broken, too.

You love her. She knows this. She loves you, too. Your mother-friend will appreciate your best efforts one day—maybe just not in the moment. Don't take anything she says personally. She's not exactly a picture of emotional or hormonal clarity right now.

You'll be great with her. From my heart and hers, thank you for reading how to understand where she's coming from.

We appreciate you. May the God of all wisdom and comfort be with you and infuse you with the gift of comfort. The Lord be with you.

Other Books by Samantha Evans

"You Are Not Alone: Grieve with Hope" Book Series

Love Letters to Miscarriage Moms: You Are Not Alone: Unprepared for reality's painful jolt, miscarriage catapulted Samantha Evans into a dark space. Sam shares her journey through loss and comes alongside you, as you find your way through heartbreak, confusion, and loneliness. This ten-year anniversary edition validates and encourages moms who find themselves awake in a pregnancy loss nightmare.

Bible Study: Who Is God in the Midst of Miscarriage Mourning? You Are Not Alone: This 13-week "You Are Not Alone" Bible study contains scripture-based love letters from God to a grieving daughter. Bible verses reveal God's comforting words in your mourning. Includes space to reflect, react, record, rest, and respond to what God's words say to your heart about healing and guidance. This study also incorporates music for a broken heart that's available on YouTube or iTunes. Release Date: Winter, 2023

Writing Journal: Love Letters to Miscarriage Moms Journal: You Are Not Alone: This standalone writing journal is for your personal use. Or it can be used by readers of *You Are Not Alone: Love Letters to Miscarriage Moms* to process your thoughts and feelings as you find your way through heartbreak, confusion, and loneliness. Release Date: Winter, 2023

Box Set: Love Letters to Miscarriage Moms: You Are Not Alone The box set includes the book, *You Are Not Alone: Love Letters to Miscarriage Moms,* the Bible Study and a Celebration Retreat. Release Date: Spring, 2023

The Rocky Path of Mourning: Navigating the Loss of a Loved One From beloved wife to single-again mom of three, Sam imparts her rocky pathway through loss, while coming alongside you in midst of the fog of mourning. Release Date: Spring, 2023

The Rocky Path of Mourning: Navigating the Loss of a Loved One— Retreat Journal This companion retreat journal records participants thoughts and feelings during Samantha Evan's *You Are Not Alone Grief Retreat.* For those who cannot attend Evans' retreat, the retail price of this retreat journal will include access to Sam's live-recorded videos from all 5 sessions. To obtain the access code to the videos, email Sam@LoveSamEvans.com Video Release Date: Spring, 2023

The Rocky Path of Mourning: Navigating the Loss of a Loved One—Writing Journal This writing journal is a standalone journal for personal use, or can be used by readers of *The Rocky Path of Mourning* to process your thoughts and feelings as you navigate the loss of a loved one. Release Date: Spring, 2023

The Adventure Devos Book Series

Adventure Devos: The first devotional written exclusively for men with a heart for risk and danger Unless it's immoral, unethical, illegal, or life-threatening, say "yes" to the adventure of life. This conversational devotional about real-life ventures addresses escape plans for temptation, appreciating women, handling change, and encouraging others. Along with perspectives on God, self-control, purpose, fear, humility, and needing Scripture, these devos all come together alongside fire-starting, runaway horses, and blood-sucking leeches.

Adventure Devos: Women's Edition: An exciting devotional written exclusively for women with a Heart for Risk and Adventure Tighten up those ponytails ladies, because mornings in God's Word just got a little more dangerous. If you crave biking, rafting, climbing, caving, surfing waves, or rappelling off cliffs, you'll enjoy this devotional about the simple moments in life, loving your family, and swift-water rescue. We dare you to take on the challenging, everyday applications that relate to the truths revealed.

Adventure Devos: Youth Edition: Summer Camp never has to end when your devotional takes you adventuring all year long This adventure devotional for teenagers illustrates Biblical truths, Godly wisdom, and life application through the lens of adrenaline-rushed ventures. Geared towards teenagers who love adventure, the excitement of summer camp just came to everyday life.

Other Books By Blackside Publishing

The Orphan Maker's Sin, **Holly DeHerrera** Fifteen years have passed since a car bomb blew up seven-year-old Ella's father, a colonel in the Air Force. One minute her daddy was there. The next? He disappeared, leaving only a charred shell of a vehicle and a burnt hubcap clacking down a Turkish street. Gone. As if he never existed at all.

The percussion of her father's violent death still ricochets in the present. Ella yearns for healing and peace from the emotional shrapnel embedded in her heart. Drawn back to Turkey—a place she swore she left behind—Ella seeks to solve the mystery of who killed her father—and why.

When she meets Murat, a handsome Turkish man, she almost hopes for a new beginning—until she discovers family secrets that torture Murat and shake Ella to her core. Will the war in her soul close her heart to receive or give love—or forgiveness?

Ella faces two choices. Stay anchored to a bitter past or seek a new ending. Can Ella move past old wounds? Or, is the damage too shattering, making healing impossible?

The Middlebury Mystery Book Series, Holly DeHerrera for Ages 7-11 includes:

Middlebury Mystery Book Club Questions. A closed Facebook group, Middlebury Mystery Book Club, to provide homeschoolers, teachers, tutors, and grandparents with ideas to inspire great conversations about this mystery series and to explore important life-application principles. 3-D Reading Activities for Homeschoolers and Creative Parents. Old-Timey Mennonite recipes in *The Root Cellar Mystery*.

The Root Cellar Mystery, **Holly Yoder DeHerrera:** Old Order Mennonite cousins, Poppy and Sadie, suspect "A re-e-a-a-al criminal" is staying at Aendi Hannah's bed and breakfast. A missing dog, a mysterious code, creepy creaks, and a floating light in the dark of night only make Poppy and Sadie more jumpy and suspicious of their strange, elderly guest.

After spotting wads of green bills in the snowy headed guest's large trunk, the sleuthing cousins wonder: *Was Ms. Lindy just released from prison and is she a thief?* To figure out what this little old, Mennonite grandmother is up to, the junior detectives spy on their mysterious guest. Confused by Ms. Lindy's odd behavior and an accidental discovery in an old-timey recipe journal, the nosy amateur sleuths hit a dead end. *Why has Ms. Lindy come to Middlebury, Indiana, and what is the puzzling stranger searching for in Aendi Hannah's root cellar?* Will Poppy and Sadie's snoopery solve the mystery surrounding Ms. Lindy's past in this cozy mystery in the children's Middlebury Mystery series?

The Key in the Wall Mystery, **Holly Yoder DeHerrera:** A bad back laid up energetic Aendi Hannah, who's likely going stir crazy. Poppy and Sadie fix up the rooms for guests staying at the Aendi Hannah's bed and breakfast in Middlebury, Indiana. While cleaning, Poppy and Sadie discover a key behind a broken baseboard in the guesthouse. *Who hid the key that looks like a skeleton's bony finger, and why?*

Their crazy quilt clues—an old cast iron key, 70-year-old letters promising a great treasure, a lost, buried time capsule, and a hidden, secret room—lay out no real pattern or direction. Like the back burner on Aendi Hannah's big, old gas stove, the trail grows cold.

Twelve-year-old, amateur sleuth Poppy worries: Will their snoopery discover any new leads to follow? And how will the Old Order Mennonite, junior detectives find time to solve this mystery while attending school, cooking meals, and taking care of a household, plus guests? Are the mystifying lock and treasure lost forever? Or are Poppy and Sadie on a wild goose chase in this cozy mystery in the children's Middlebury Mystery series?

The Covered Bridge Mystery, **Holly Yoder DeHerrera:** What kind of creep lurks just waiting to steal from Mammi or Dawdi? Poppy and Sadie never expected a real, honest-to-goodness burglar to strike in their close-knit, Old Order Mennonite community in Middlebury, Indiana. The pie-swiping culprit mystifies everyone by stashing all the stolen evidence inside the dusky-dark, covered bridge near Dawdi's farm.

Is the thief-on-the-loose tempting the suspicious cousins to catch him—or her? Jonah, who's developmentally disabled and distraught, fears the burglar will hurt his grandparents. And to make matters worse, Mammi and Dawdi refuse to lock their barn and house—even at night. Using an apple pie as bait, the junior detectives set a trap.

Will these amateur sleuths nab the criminal or will the bandit remain on the run in this cozy mystery in the children's Middlebury Mystery series?

For Middle School and High Schoolers: *A Multi-Genre Teen Writing Curriulum,* **Holly DeHerrera**

Too often Holly DeHerrera hears kids say, "I hate writing." Or parents say, "I'm so frustrated. I have to force my child to write."

Your child can discover the power of language and the joy of writing. Writing involves far more than mastering the mechanics. Like that old saying, "Putting the cart before the horse," if a student doesn't love writing, or entertain at least a joyful tolerance, stressing rules without free expression chokes imaginative creativity and critical thinking skills.

A student's ability to write affects student achievement in all subject areas. *Unleash the Pen, A Multi-Genre Teen Writing Curriculum* ignites a love for writing and self-expression through words. DeHerrera's plan to teach writing combines writing instruction with diverse, creative writing projects.

Students dive into a topic of their choosing, while experimenting with a variety of fun writing assignments with authentic connections to their lives and their studies. Each self-guided, creative writing incentive leads the student to learn by writing.

Unleash the Pen, A Multi-Genre Teen Writing Curriculum is designed for tweens and teens to independently work at their own pace, or over the course of a 36-week school year. This teacher-friendly, multi-genre curriculum motivates your students to leap into the adventure of writing. Available Spring, 2023.

The Red Menace, **Jeff Kildow, Historical Fiction**

A sadistic KGB assassin.

A dozen atomic bombs.

The world can only hope Col. Joel Knight's mission succeeds.

Dateline: Norton Air Force Base, 14 July 1950—The Soviets protest AF pilot Col. Joel Knight's nomination as the Aviation Attaché to Moscow. Joel faces a demotion or a forced resignation—until—Major General Garret "Red" McNeil offers Joel a temporary 'piece of cake' assignment with the CIA . . . a "flying job, pure and simple."

Joel's mission? Fly undercover to China as a WWII war veteran pilot-for-hire in a converted Navy Lockheed PV-2 Harpoon and extract a defecting Russian atomic scientist. If captured, Knight will be shot as a spy. Meanwhile in the Kremlin, Deputy Chairman of the Council of People's Commissars, Beria plots to unleash A-bombs on U.S. and U.N. troops in Korea and blame China.

The CIA's complicated evacuation plan backfires. A high-stakes getaway-turned-deadly endangers the lives of not one, but six Russian scientists, plus their CIA rescuers. A run-for-their-lives pursuit by the ruthless KGB plunges the fugitives into a nail-biting race against time in the Siberian wilderness. The against-all-odds mission tests Joel's skills as a leader and a pilot. If Joel fails—all will die.

Knight joins forces with an unlikely ally—a secretive, Mongolian collective farm commissar. As the clock counts down . . . will the three-way one-upmanship between the Soviets, the Mongolians, and the Americans result in a daring escape or death? Will Joel reach General Douglas MacArthur in time to convince the stubborn, five-star general to evacuate before the Russians launch their full-scale atomic attacks?

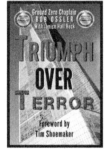 ***Triumph Over Terror*, Ground Zero Chaplain Bob Ossler with Janice Hall Heck. Foreword by Tim Shoemaker**

When terrorism, politics, and violence lunges too far, heroes arise. What happens when an ordinary American shows up in Manhattan after the worst terror attack on American soil since Pearl Harbor?

The day that changed the world—September 11, 2001—propelled America into the long war, the Global War on Terror. Like many Americans who serve our country, Chaplain Bob Ossler donned his firefighter turn-out gear, boarded a plane, and made his way to Manhattan to help in any way possible. He was escorted onto the smoldering, quaking heap, dubbed "The Pile." Entering into the Gates of Hell—the crematorium and morgue for nearly 3000 beloved souls—an electrifying chill of horror shot through him.

Trained as a professional first responder, Ossler served five tours of duty during the cleanup at Ground Zero after 9/11. Bob's eyewitness vignettes recount the questions, fears, struggles, and sacrifices of the families and workers overwhelmed by despair. Chaplain Ossler conducted over 300 mini-memorials for the fragmentary remains carried off the Pile. He comforted the mourners, the frightened, and the heartbroken laborers sifting through millions of tons of carnage for the remains of their friends, the unknown dead—and their faith.

From the broken fragments of glass, steel, and men, Chaplain Ossler's mosaic of God's grace unveils the outpouring of generosity, heroism, and unity from people who stepped up to do "something." Ossler honors the ultimate sacrifice and bravery of first responders who rush toward terror to save lives.

Chaplain Ossler chronicles the best of humanity—acts of courage and goodness in the midst of chaos, personal tragedy, and unimaginable devastation. As terrorist attacks continue to assault humanity, Ossler reveals how your spirit can triumph over terror's reign, and how you can help others suffering from trauma and loss.

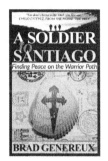

A Soldier to Santiago: Finding Peace on the Warrior Path, **Brad Genereux. Foreword by Heather A. Warfield, Ph.D. Afterword by Dr. Christine Bridges Esser**

"I gave the best years of my life to a cause—to a belief that proved false. I loved living on the edge. The thrill of standing the watch. Rushing into harm's way on behalf of my country. For over 22 years and with pride, I represented America by wearing the cloth of the nation. When my service was all over? *Life had passed me by and . . . I fit in—nowhere."—Senior Chief Petty Officer Brad Genereux.*

Is forgiveness and peace within the grasp of those who spent their lives pursuing the next mission on behalf of their country? Brad Genereux traces two parallel journeys—one through the inferno of war in Afghanistan, and the other through the healing purgatory of the Camino de Santiago. Juxtaposed between a combat zone and The Way of Saint James, experience two adventures and the two lives of one man. Willing to sacrifice his life to aid the Afghanis, Brad's candid account chronicles the challenges to carry out missions while operating under a complex chain of command, Afghani corruption, and deadly sabotage by the Taliban.

After Genereux retired from the military, he faced the arduous pursuit to assimilate into civilian life and to make sense of the unexpected deaths of three family members. Brad revisits dark demons imprisoning his spirit and the healing peace unlocked on The Way of Saint James. This book shadows the reflections of a war-hardened man devoid of identity and purpose and his search for answers, hope, and himself on a 769-kilometer trek over the Pyrenees and across northern Spain.

Are you searching for peace and purpose? Are you suffering from hypervigilance, isolation, nightmares, or insomnia? Experience the camaraderie of warriors deployed to the battlefield and the esprit de corps of Camino peregrinos as they triumph over the inner battles of the spirit.

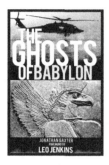

The Ghosts of Babylon, Jonathan Baxter. Foreword by Leo Jenkins *The haunting poetry of The Ghosts of Babylon is as near to the crucible of war as you can get without wearing Kevlar and camouflage.*

Every war triggers the question—what's war like? *The Ghosts of Babylon* offers eyewitness accounts. Warriors lost their innocence dueling in the sands of the Iraqi inferno, or fighting in the chilling Afghan mountains or on the khaki-colored plains. Wounds enshrouded under the bandages of headlines and sound bites never bridge the gap between soldier and civilian.

Only a soldier poet lays bare the honor and horror. Only a veteran reveals the physical and mental battles waged by the warrior caste. Only the war poet distills the emotions of those who tasted bravery and terror, love and vengeance, life and death. Based on the experiences of a U.S. Army Ranger turned private security contractor, these powerful poems capture the essence of Jonathan Baxter's twelve military and civilian deployments.

Jonathan reveals the contradictory nature of deployment in a war zone—exhilaration, monotony, ugliness, and occasional beauty. From ancient times to present day, war poetry telegraphs a dispatch across the ages about the universal experiences of war—brotherhood and bereavement, duty and disillusionment, and heroism and horror. No history mirrors the brutal realities and emotions of armed conflict more than the shock of war erupting from the warrior poet's pen.

Jonathan resurrects the ghosts and gods of soldiers past. His poignant memorial to fallen brothers transmits the shadowy presence and ultimate sacrifices of the unfortunate coffined to the fortunate un-coffined. *The Ghosts of Babylon* strips away the cultural varnish of the 'enemy,' and paints the bitter irony of every day lives trapped in the crosshairs of terror, chaos, and death. From moving to startling to soulful, these masterpieces provoke you to think about the truths and consequences of those who risk their lives on the frontline of freedom—for you, their friends, and our country.